A WATCHMAN

Written by Gary Welkom

Edited by Charity Townsend

ISBN 979-8-88685-486-2 (paperback)
ISBN 979-8-88685-487-9 (digital)

Christian Faith Publishing
832 Park Avenue
Meadville, PA 16335
www.christianfaithpublishing.com

Printed in the United States of America

This book is written and dedicated to my
grandmother Bessie Brassington.
Bessie was a very strong person, not only in life but also in spirit.
She loved the Lord with all her heart, as we should.
She often spoke in tongues when she prayed.
She held the whole family together. God's peaceful spirit
surrounded her at all times. It seemed as though all things
fell in order around her, as only the spirit of God can do.
It is because of her that this book is being written, to let all who
read this know what her message was and how it will soon affect us.

If only I could reach your level of love and peace,
the struggle would be well worth it.
God bless you, Bessie.

Contents

Introduction

In Ezekiel 33:3–7, God states the following:

> If the watchman seeth the sword come upon the land, he blows the trumpet and warn the people. Then whosoever heareth the sound of the trumpet and taketh not warning, if the sword come and take him away, his blood shall be upon his own head. He heard the sound of the trumpet and took not warning. His blood shall be upon him. But he that taketh warning shall deliver his soul. But if the watchman sees the sword come and blow not the trumpet, and the people be not warned, if the sword come and take any person from among them, he is taken away in his iniquity, but his blood will I require at the watchman's hand. So thou, o son of man, I have set thee a watchman unto the house of Israel. Therefore, thou shall hear the word at my mouth, and warn them from me.

These words should have a special meaning to all who believe in Christ, for we are all watchmen in the eyes of God. I've finally come to understand what God would have me do: Witness to all who will listen, for the time is short. To tell of God's love for us and his precious forgiveness, which is open to all of us that not one should perish but have everlasting life.

In the pages to come, I will try to explain my life of love, lone-liness, hatred, and finally salvation, and of the mistakes I made and God's forgiveness of them.

The Farm

THE VERY BEGINNING WAS ONE of love for all things, people, and animals. I guess I'd have to start this story riding in the wagon with my older brother, Tom. He sat on one side of the rear of the wagon and I on the other. Our job was to pull off the corn husks that were still attached to the cobs of corn. I don't really think we were expected to get a lot done, but it gave us something to do while our mother plucked the corn, running from row to row and tossing them in the wagon. Pa drove, of course, slowly so Ma had time to get all the corn in a number of rows. I showed my stubbornness as I struggled with a tough cob of corn; finally, Ma came to help. It seemed so easy for her.

At the house, our main entertainment was to listen as Ma read us books on the couch. Pa and Ma had placed a large blanket across the kitchen entrance. Even though I didn't know why at the time, it finally dawned on me. It was to keep the cold out. As Ma would read, all of a sudden, a mouse trap would go off. Wow! We got one! We'd run in and see what we'd caught. This seemed to go on night after night. I guess we had a lot of mice. What did send shivers down my spine were the thousand-leggers that ran across the floor. They sure could move; even Ma would jump up. A shoe was a very good weapon if you could catch them before they disappeared. Even with all of this, these were good times.

From what I hear, we were a handful, Tom and I. We had a large place to roam on the farm. There was a small porch on the rear of the house, and someone had left paint in cans there. Somehow, we got the cans open and were sliding around naked in the paint. Oh, what a mess we must have been. Our past time consisted of riding hay bales down the chute to the barnyard. We also got a kick out of jumping on the pigs for a ride, and what a ride it was. Of course, Ma took us to church on Sundays. Bessie was alive at the time, and our relations also went. Pa was from a Catholic family, and Ma from a Pentecostal one. There were two people who spoke in tongues there, and Bessie was one of them. It seemed I was always analytical and tried to figure out what they were saying but had no luck, of course. Then one day, we got a TV in the house. It was black and white back then, but we didn't mind. We were told it was a sin to watch it, though, so I'd run by it, trying not to look. Now that I think back on it, if it were a sin, why did they get one? Then one night, I had a very vivid dream. Our house sat below the barn with a few sheds around it. In this dream, I had stepped outside and started walking toward the barn. All of a sudden, a loud voice called my name. The ground was shaking terribly. I was terrified and started running back to the house. The dream was short but left me with a shaken memory. It seemed so real. The next day, I told ma. "You should have asked what he wanted," she replied.

A well-known preacher was coming to a town about thirty miles away. I believe his name was Grant, but I could be mistaken. Ma, Bessie, and the rest of the family went to see him. I don't remember Pa going, although my aunts and uncles did. I was standing next to Bessie, and a bunch of other people were standing there as well. They started talking in tongues and had their arms raised in the air. I stood there bewildered, a little kid looking up to see what all the fuss was about. A large cloud of smoke started to come over us from the rear of the building. Looking up front, I saw a man motion for another, who came up to him. I figured the man must be in some kind of authority, as the other had come when called. Watching this, he sent the man to the rear of the building with the motion of his hand. I started watching him go from one door to another. He'd go in and check for something and do the next. When he was done, he went up to the other and shrugged his shoulders. It occurred to me then that he'd been checking for a fire. I didn't know it at the time that not everyone saw it. The man up front had seen it, though, or he wouldn't have done what he had. I know now it was the Holy Ghost.

As time went by, it turned out I was very timid and shy. The girls on the school bus would tease me every time I got on. Finally, I asked loudly, of course, "Why do you all do this?" "It's fun" was their reply. "It's not fun to me," I said. This seemed to quell the teasing for the most part. One day, I got a duck, a baby duck, that is. It must have been a holiday or something. Of course, I sure loved that little duck. It seemed he got lonely in the cardboard box, so I put him upon the bed with me one night. In the morning, to my horror, he was dead, stiff as a board. This really broke my heart, and I cried my heart out. It was my fault he was dead, as I must have rolled on him. Ma just smiled and gave me a shoe box to bury him in.

On the farm, we had one milk cow, wouldn't you know her name was Bessie, which Pa would milk every day. There were other cows, but they didn't give milk. Pa really liked this cow, you could tell. One day, she had a baby calf, and she died giving birth. I remember her turning her head back and looking at her calf; a tear ran down her face, and she was gone. Animals must have feelings too. As it turned out, Pa said to me, "This will be your calf, if you feed it." So every morning and afternoon, I'd mix up a bucket of calf feed for the calf. The bucket had a big nipple on it so the calf would drink through it. Then one day after school, I went to feed it, and it was gone. Again, I was brokenhearted and started crying for it. Ma and Pa said it just walked up on the truck. They'd loaded another cow on the truck at the time. I'm not sure where it went but probably to the market. I never saw it again. As a matter of fact, it seemed even if you bought a calf from Pa, it never seemed to grow. It defied the law of nature. Within a few years, I caught on and traded Tom a calf for his pig when the pigs went to market. That was it for my raising of any animals on the farm. I still had to work the farm though.

As time went by, I started to realize that our house was not normal. We had a long dirt road to the house. As soon as you pulled in the driveway, the house came into view even though it seemed a quarter mile off. Sometimes our lights would be on as we turned onto the driveway. Somebody's home was our reply. Pa usually was not with us. He seemed to stay around the farm quite a bit. He had a daytime job, and the farm to kept him busy. As we pulled next to the house, the lights would be off. Tom and I would check all the doors and windows to no avail. It seemed the house was empty and all secure. Something wasn't right about it, as I was to find out later.

As time went by, Tom and I grew, of course. When we'd get in trouble, of course, we'd get spanked. My brother told me, "When they hit ya, cry and run." I just couldn't act at all. The pain would have to get bad enough to bring real tears. I must have seemed defiant right from the start. In later years, I did get defiant, and with a vengeance. Tom had gotten very sick when he was young and had a heart murmur. He still does today. So when it came to farm labor, I got the heavier jobs. To get to school, we walked from the house through a small wooded area and across the field, past the neighbors' house and then to the highway. Someone had built us a little shack to sit in while we waited on the bus. Tom, Randy, and I could hide from the weather in it. Randy was the neighbor kid. Later in years, Pa also farmed their land. We were to hear how great of a kid Randy was compared to us for quite a while.

The farm was spread across a valley, which had a fence row (a row of trees with a fence on the eastern end) out to the hard road. This fence row ran from east to west and ended up below the pond Pa had built. The pond was fed by a little stream, if you want to call it that. When it was almost completed, Tom and I were playing around it. On the far side was an opening in the bank of the pond. Tom being one year older than I, jumped across to the other side. He made it across just fine. When I tried, I fell right into the mudhole, which the outpouring water had made. This is where I got into trouble. I kept sinking and could not get out. Tom kept trying to pull me out by the hair. All he'd get was another handful of hair. Finally, he ran to the house, which was just up the hill a little bit. Ma came down with him to pull me out. I was in up to my chest and still going down. From what I hear, Ma lost her shoes getting me out of there. When I think about it, what a way to go. After the pond was finished and full of water, I almost drowned by stepping into a hole. All I heard was Ma screaming when I went under as she had been sitting on the bank. Green is all I remember seeing at the time. Pa must have pulled me out, although I don't know to this day.

Bessie would come out to the farm now and then. I remember her helping Ma with the dishes. I was alone with Bessie for some reason. Ma and everyone else had gone somewhere. I was still pretty young at the time, so she must have been watching me. Bessie called me to come to her. When I did, she took me to the side. "There's something I want you to look out for," she said. "A one-world government and one church. This is the beginning of the end of the world." For some reason, these words Bessie spoke stayed with me the rest of my life. Now I know she must have been speaking in the Spirit because I've never forgotten those words.

As time passed, things changed around the farm. Pa started to get mean and did a lot of screaming at us. When Tom and I would see him driving down the dirt road, we'd go hide in the cornfield. We knew we'd be in for a lot of cursing and screaming. "Where do you go, what do you do? You'll have to come back sometime!" This always stuck in my mind. Fear just gripped me. Living in fear just saps all the strength out of you. As it turned out, the fear of him was only part of the problem. Something was in the house. I could feel it when I took a shower down the cellar. It always seemed you were being watched. The place started to give me the creeps. The barn was different. I'd play there for hours. I took an old broomstick and sharpened the tip. For a weight, I twisted a large nut on the sharp end. This made a good spear. I could stab bales as they were the enemy. It would stick when thrown because of the weight on the end. I'd heard a rumor someone had seen people hanging in the barn, though I'd never seen anyone. It sure felt a lot safer than the house.

I thought about Pa screaming all the time. Maybe if I helped Ma with the housework, I could put her in a good mood, and Pa wouldn't scream at us. Of course, this didn't work no matter how I tried. I had a place of refuge. It was quite a ways from the house, down in the woods. It was a different place from the rest of the woods. Usually, if you sat still in the woods, animals would start to move around ya. Not so in my refuge spot. Animals didn't seem to come around as in other places. It was a little valley, which ran into the major one from the north side. The main valley ran east to west. Something else that was odd about the place was there were pits of some sort on the sides of the valley. You'd have thought a tree had blown down and uprooted, although no trees were lying there or any sign of them. It would have been a perfect ambush spot. Pine trees dotted each side of the valley. I'd sit under a pine tree and think about Pa and what I must have been doing wrong to bring his anger upon me as it was. I also thought about ending it all, right then and there. I had a rifle with me usually when I went into the woods. The more I thought about it, the more I was convinced that if I were to go out, I would go out swinging. Make a difference in this world.

We didn't eat together often, except on Sunday. Another thing I didn't understand. I would be at the dinner table at times and would know what someone was going to say before they said it, as though I'd lived it before. I knew the outcome would end in a big fight. If I had said something and moved or walked in any certain direction, I'd change it to try and throw off the outcome. It never did work though. It always ended badly and made me feel helpless.

I had another real problem and still have it today. I'm a lousy liar. You can see it in my face. Why lie, you'll get caught anyway. Ma knew this and would ask me things at times. Of course, it would be the truth. There are times when you need to say nothing, although it took me a while to learn this. This got me in trouble with my brother Tom and various friends who came over once in a while. I started to get picked on because of this. Being timid and overly shy, I started to withdraw from crowds. There was a cousin of mine named Jim who was my age. We'd been in the hospital together when we got our tonsils out. He never put me down for anything, and we started to get real close. Although I didn't know it at the time, he was shy also. I'd walk or ride my bike over to his house, which was probably four miles away. He had a rocket set, which we had a lot of fun with. The rockets would really fly up in the air. We then caught a mouse and put him in the clear tube that was just behind the nose of the rocket. We launched, and he flew out of sight. After a minute or two, we'd see the parachute open on the rocket and float down to the ground. We then retrieved it and took out the mouse. He didn't look hurt at all. He did move real slow though. We let him go after that. He'd earned it. Later on, Jim and I were older and were hunting on the farm. It was small game season at the time. I was a little ahead of Jim as we walked back toward the house on the farm. All of a sudden, I heard someone's voice, which sounded like Pa's, say there's a pheasant. Looking to my right, I see three guys pull up their shotguns. In my mind, I think they were not going to shoot. They did! I froze, and Jim threw a body block, which knocked my legs out from under me. As I fell flat on my back, I could see the shot tear the brush I'd been standing in front of. If it hadn't been for Jim, I'd have been in real trouble. I yelled at the three to stop firing, which they did.

As time went by, for some reason, his mom would be yelling at us, telling him to get away from me because I was no good. I didn't know why or what I'd done. To this day, I'm still not sure. I can only speculate. Something did come to light later on in time, although it might have been a different reason. Pa would always go to people and say we never helped him do anything. They, of course, believed him. Why would he lie? The truth was we were little more than slaves. Tom and I were to pick up hay bales in the field while Pa was at work. We were too small to pick them up and started crying. We knew we were in for it if we could not get it done. So we got Ma to help. She couldn't pick them up either. This saved us, as it wasn't for lack of trying. We never knew when he'd come home pissed off, although we'd know by how he drove. I didn't know it at that time, but the neighbor could hear him screaming at us from the next farm. I got to feed the cattle before school and after. I also had furnace duty to fill the coal hopper and take out the ashes.

This was a normal day, and it got real intense in the summer. Lots of lawn to mow and hay to bale. I was born to stack hay, or so it seemed. In later years, we farmed our 120 acres and sharecropped two other farms next to us. There were times when Tom and I would get in an argument while working on the hay wagon over who would stack and who would pull the hay onto the wagon. If Pa had to stop baling, he'd come back to the wagon. Tom would jump off and run. I was thinking, *Where do you go? You'll have to come back some day.* I'd stay on the wagon and back up as far as I could. The outcome was always the same. I'd get punched in the face and fall off the wagon. I would wipe the blood off and get back to work. It's back to stacking.

I should know not to do it again. Somehow, it just didn't seem fair, so I'd get in another argument later on with the same result. I couldn't seem to figure it out, I guess. Walking home from the school bus stop, I'd get put in the field to work. Tom carried my books to the house for me. Through all this, I still had a lot of love in my heart. Jim and I would get together and do something when we could. We had fun just sharing our time together.

My brother Tom and I got to join the Boy Scouts. It seemed to be a lot of fun, and I would recommend it to children today. The camping was the most fun to me. We got to go on a weekend camping trip. I can't remember the name of the place anymore. Anyway, we had no sleeping bags of our own. Grandpa Welkom loaned us one, said we could both fit in it. Wouldn't you know, only one of us could fit. Tom being the oldest got the sleeping bag. Someone loaned me a blanket. It sure got cold at camp that night. I woke up not knowing where I was or if I was in the tent or outside of it. Someone had a huge fire going, so I stood by it and shivered till morning. The next day, we had a lot of fun because we got into a rock fight with another bunch of scouts across the stream. They had pits to hide in, which we didn't have. They didn't seem to understand that we knew how to lob the rocks over the stream and into the pits in which they were hiding. We were winning until the high brass caught us throwing rocks. Fun was over, and we now had enemies across the stream. That night didn't seem as cold as the last one had been. We rolled up camp the next day, which probably was a good thing. My brother Tom finally decided to quit scouts. I tried to keep going there until, one day, the scoutmaster showed up and asked Pa for some money. I don't think it was a lot, twelve dollars at the time, but Pa sure got pissed. We'd been filling in a bridge with rocks at the time when the scoutmaster showed up. Cursing at me, Pa told me to fill the whole bridge in with rocks and not come up to the house until done. I was in tears while I kept trying to fill in the bridge. It was impossible to finish. It got very dark, but I still tried to work. Finally, Pa came down, yelled some more, and told me to get up the house. That was it for the scouts. From then on, I was done with it. It wasn't worth all the yelling.

Time went by, and we were in high school. Southern Area High was our school. When I first stepped into the place, I was nervous. Everyone was busy running around. I didn't know anyone in particular at the time to run around with. Our school had a couple choices of classes you could belong to—agriculture, shop, business, and of course, academic. Our shop class had two shops, carpentry and metal fabrication. All of the above did not fit where my interest lay. Mechanics was my thing. I liked to take things apart. I didn't always get them back together though. I tried all of them for a period of time, even academic for a day. French went right over my head. I'm sure the rest of it would have too. I'm not sure how long I stayed in each of the other classes. Because of my lack of interest, I started skipping classes. Tom, Ray, Mike, and I would go to the woods and take hikes. I asked the principal if he could get me in a tech school, which was in Bloomsburg, Pennsylvania. His answer was, "Not even." It seemed I'd pissed him off because he told me I couldn't even see a counselor. After that, I could not care less about the school. There was a dance at the school one night. Tom and our friends didn't want to stay, so they went out drinking. As shy as I was, two girls were trying to teach me how to dance. It was fun, but when it was over, my brother never showed up to pick me up. The reason was he'd been in a wreck on the way to get me. He'd run a stop sign and got hit broadside. He was in the hospital. When I saw his car, it made me sick to my stomach. Later on, I was wishing I had been with him. Pa just kept yelling at me about being at the dance. If you focus on one spot, you can still hear them yell, but it would seem far away.

Tom, our friend Mike, and I had skipped school and were walking down by my grandfather's place along the road. All of a sudden, Tom and Mike took off running. Of course, I had to turn around to see what was behind us. Just in time to catch a right hook, I flew over the bank from the impact. Pa jumped down and pinned me down to the ground and just beat me bloody. Later he dragged me to Grandpa's and chased me upstairs to get cleaned up. My grandparents yelled at him for beating me bloody.

I really liked history class and would try to get homework done for it. I had very little time for schoolwork anyway. I was working the fields till dark. Like I said, I'd give my brother my books and have to go out in the field right after school. It would be dark by the time I finished in the fields, and then there was the furnace to check on. It didn't use a lot of coal in the summertime, but it also heated our water. This made it an all-year job.

I was fifteen when I quit school, on a farm release sort of thing. Of course, I had help from the principal at the school. Tom had quit also, of course; he was sixteen at the time. It seemed as soon as I woke up and got coffee, there would be a note on the table. This note would tell me all the things I needed to have done by the time Pa got home. It was impossible to get them done in one day and, many times, totally impossible for one person to do at all. There were times Ma and Tom would be leaving to go somewhere, and Ma would ask if I wanted to go. Of course, I couldn't. I was terrified what would happen if the impossible was not completed. More than once I'd end up not finished and it would be night. No one else would be at home, and then I had to deal with the terror to come. If I was upstairs, it would sound as though the chairs were moving in the kitchen. Downstairs, the furniture upstairs would make noise. I couldn't win for losing. I'd been taught if someone breaks in the house to shoot them. If they fall out the window, throw them back in. One night, I was sitting there watching TV. I was scared, so I had the rifle across my lap as I sat there. The living room had a closet, which was at the top of the stairs, leading to the basement. This meant it had two doors. One opened up to the closet and the other to the stairway to the basement. Even with the TV on, I could hear someone walking up the stairs and hear the basement door open. To my horror, the door to the living room opened about six inches. Sweat was running down my face as I trembled in fear. Rifle at the ready, two things were going through my mind. *If I fire and I'm nuts, man, I am going to get it when Pa gets home. If this thing is a ghost or demon, how will I stop it anyway?* Finally, the stress was too much. Outside I ran. Once there, I tried to find what I felt was a safe spot in the lawn. I wandered around in the dark. For some reason, I found a spot that felt safe, or at least defendable. Someone finally showed up. We looked for someone in the house but found none. There was something else going on in the house at the time. While I'd be sleeping, or should I say trying to, I'd hear one too many breathing patterns. To explain this, it seemed you could hear everyone's breathing, which was not quite a snore. I'd lie there and add them up. Always one too many, which was in my room. At first, you try to think it's just your imagination until it gets worst, then comes the smell of what seemed like rotten meat. Ma also smelled it. She got me a cross and told me to say the words (in Jesus's name, be gone). Little did I know just how powerful those words are. Later in life, I was to use them again.

Tom and I would go over to this town called Mt. Carmel, where we had a few women friends. One night, we decided to give them a scare. We'd heard about this place called White Cross. I can't remember where the place was right now, but we went there first to make sure we knew where it was. Tom drove, of course, as I was too young to drive at the time. Sure enough, there it was as soon as we pulled into the graveyard—a cross, big and bright, right at the entrance. Off we went to get the girls. When we got back, there was no cross there. I knew I just saw it there. I got out of the car and walked over to where I'd seen the cross. I found a stump of concrete there in the tall grass. I put my hands on it and started feeling around the top of it. All of a sudden, it came to my mind. This is way old, as the concrete was very crumbly. No one had just taken it; it was weathered. "Ah… let's get out of here quick," I said as I jumped back in the car. Away we went with the only one spooked being me.

I was fifteen when I got a job in the grainery. I forged my working papers to make it look as though I was sixteen. Ma had to drive me to work until I turned sixteen. It was a dusty, hard job, and when I got off from work, I was dead on my feet. For the first two weeks, I would crawl into the pond to get most of the dust off and then take a shower. Soon, I was back in the field after work until dark. There were no breaks, not even on the weekends. The sun comes up, you start work and work till dark. The sun came up right on the fence row, which was exactly east, and went down on the west side. Many years later, I was to see that change when I returned and found that the sun's position had come up by the neighbor's instead of the fence row. A preacher also noticed that the sun wasn't coming up in the same place and said something terrible was going to happen.

After I'd turned sixteen, the folks decided it was time for me to get a vehicle. I'm sure Ma was tired of taking me to work. The car they chose for me was a big four-door Plymouth. It sure wasn't a kid's car. They probably figured I'd get in a wreck like my brother. Going from work to work five days a week and all weekend on the farm started to get to me. Even your mule needs a break at least one day a week. I started running that car at high speeds everywhere I went. One day, I was driving from the mill to the house. The highway was four lanes in one place as you topped the hill coming from Catawissa to a place called Slabtown. This is where my grandparents on the Welkom side lived. The highway has an intersection with two small roads intersecting it. I think I was running around 90 mph down this road. There was a flatbed truck in the passing lane. I was traveling in the slow lane to the far right. As I was about to pass the truck, which was loaded with cement blocks, he turned from the center lane to the right, which blocked my lane. All I saw was that load of cement blocks right in front of me. I had nowhere to go and no time to do it. Everything happened so fast there was no time to react. My life passed before my eyes. To explain this, it's like right from that moment, you see everything you did in your life in fast-forward reverse. I was on the other side of the flatbed truck, without a scratch. Looking to my left, I could see another vehicle, which was on the other side of the road, getting ready to pull out on the highway. Some lady was driving, and her mouth was wide open. She'd seen what I'd missed, and she looked shocked. I kept going and never stopped. I needed to get away from there. I kept thinking about what had just happened but told no one.

Jim and I took my car and went down to see a tractor pull in Harrisburg, Pennsylvania. We had a good time there as we did just being together. On the way back, we got lost and didn't know how to get out of Harrisburg. Jim was reading the map as I drove. "Cheesetown," he said. What was my reply? "We're lost and you're reading Cheesetown," I said in a scolding tone. We laughed so bad we had tears in our eyes. This was good times, which were to change one spring day. Jim had a motorcycle, which he rode most of the time. I'd ridden with him at times. He was very good at it and explained to me about never to use the brakes hard when you get surprised by a sharp corner. Use the engine to slow yourself down instead. We had also talked about me selling my car and getting a bike so we could ride together and maybe see some country we hadn't seen as yet. One spring day, I got the news. Jim had been in an accident on his bike. He was in the hospital in bad shape. His dad was away at the time. He was in the military and was a sharpshooter for the state of Pennsylvania. My aunt had to make the decisions on what to do. Jim had been riding with a helmet on at the time. He had a bad head injury. If someone had helped him at the time, he probably would have made it. They operated on him, but he didn't make it. This was a changing point in my life. I stormed out of intensive care, pissed off. The nurses grabbed my aunt as she started to pass out. Later on, the tears came to me in floods.

That night, Pa put me to work out in the field. I can't remember if I was plowing or running the harrows. The stars were out, and I was running with the tractor lights. Tears just poured down my face. I lost track of time. The only thing on my mind was Jim. Looking up into the sky, I saw a ball of light going straight up into the heavens. I saw this through many tears. I was also a pallbearer for Jim. A strange thing happened when we carried him to the hearse. A feeling of complete peace encircled me as we slid him in. Through the whole funeral, I couldn't get that out of my mind.

My loneliness turned to anger from this point on. I was still working at the grainery, and my hair had grown longer, though it wasn't down to my shoulders or anything. On the way home, for once, I was driving slower than I usually did. I was extremely tired and not paying attention as I passed a car. It seemed I couldn't get around him. I gave it a little more speed to complete the pass. The car was still alongside me. I then tried to slow down so I could slide in behind him. He wouldn't allow this either and kept me out in the oncoming traffic lane. This continued on for about a mile, so I sped up to try to get around him. Looking down, I was doing ninety miles an hour. There was a turn coming up, and cars were just completing the turn. Choices ran through my mind: hit the cars head on or take my car over the bank into the trees. As I looked over at the car who had me in this position, the driver was looking at me, just grinning from ear to ear. With time running out and only a few car lengths to go, I chose option three. I figured he could go with me. I turned into his car, which he drove off the road and was doing 360s in a gravel lot, which belonged to the tasty freeze stand outside of Slabtown, Pennsylvania. I never did forget his face, and when Reagan became president, his picture was in the local paper. He was the local Cyclops for the KKK.

Things happened pretty fast from then on after Jim died. It had been some kind of turning point in my life for the extreme worst. Tom and I were drinking beer in Catawissa, Pennsylvania, with a few friends. We were underage, of course, and the police caught us. We hadn't been driving at the time though. As we sat in the police station, Pa came in and did something very unexpected. He stood up for us. "You don't have to stand up for me," I said with tears in my eyes. For some reason, we took off to Florida that night. Tom, Frank, and I took turns driving there.

Frank had some relation down there. That's why he lives there today. I've not seen him in years, but he's in my prayers. When we got there, the humidity was terrible. His relation was very nice to us while we were there. When the time came to leave, we gathered aluminum to sell for the gas back. The tires on the car were bad with little thread left on them, so we decided to get different ones. Frank's brother knew where a junkyard was, and we went there and stole the tires. On the way back, we got a flat. It figures; we stole the tires. They had tread on them though. The ones on the way down were bald, and we had no problems then. When we made it back, the engine in the Dodge died. Rods or main bearing, I think. It knocked something terrible. Of course, it was unusable for transportation after that.

My next vehicle was another Plymouth. I didn't really get to pick this one either, but at least it was a sporty-looking Plymouth. It was a 'Cuda two-door. It was a bright red color, and I didn't care for it much although it did look sporty. I had a job up at the dog food plant in Bloomsburg. This is where I really started to make mistakes. The job was at night from 11:00 p.m. to 7:00 a.m. I'd started smoking pot by then, and by the time 11:00 p.m. came around, I sure didn't feel like going into a factory. I also had a lot of pressure from the party crowd I hung out with at the time. Later I was to learn that I hated factory work of any kind and needed to work outside. It didn't take long to fall behind on the payments, and I sold the 'Cuda. Again, I picked up an older Plymouth, a lil' Colt. I had no payments on this one and had started working in the grainery again. It had a push-button auto shift on the dash, which I thought was cool. It kinda looked like the '57 Chevy in a way.

As things worked out, a concert by Deep Purple was to take place in Harrisburg, Pennsylvania. I had a few friends with me, and we'd decided to go see it. For some reason, we'd stopped out the farm. Ma and Pa were there, and I'd informed them where I was going. All of a sudden, Ma started screaming about me taking drugs. Why didn't I just lie and say I wouldn't go? Not me. I told the truth instead. Pa grabbed me by the hair and started punching me in the face as he swung me around and around, punching me till my face was all blood. My friends were terrified. We walked from the farm down the road through the valley, headed to Catawissa. I heard running water and searched out the stream, where I washed the blood off. My friends asked if he did that often. "Yeah," was my reply. He'd beaten me bloody before, but this time seemed more vicious.

The Street

I DON'T KNOW WHEN I retrieved the car. I'm sure it was when Pa wasn't there. That was it for me. I was working at the grainery, and I moved to Bloomsburg, Pennsylvania. There I got a room above a bar, which was twenty dollars a week. The place was pretty sad. It had an old military bed rail and one shoddy bureau to put clothes in. The shower was shared by another person who had the other room upstairs. It was pretty gross, as it needed cleaning badly. I didn't have any cleaning supplies, so it went pretty much unclean. I was sixteen at the time when I had moved in there. I'd gotten into smoking pot and trying a few pills a while back after Jim had been killed. It was soon to ramp up. I was scared of the needles I'd heard of though. Contrary to what the government was saying, people didn't usually turn into a heroin addict after smoking pot. While I was staying at the bar, someone else rented the other room. He seemed a little older than me, but he sure wanted to buddy up real fast. I don't remember his name anymore. I really didn't care what it was at the time. All he could talk about was caves and heroin and other kinds of drugs. I didn't know anything about hard drugs back then. Later on, I told a friend about him, and we sat outside to check him out. It seemed my friend thought he looked familiar but couldn't place him. Later on, it came to my friend who he was. The guy was a narcotics officer from Harrisburg, Pennsylvania. It wasn't long before I confronted the guy, and he left the bar. All I could think of was who had sent him to check on me and why. I was no dealer and didn't do hard drugs.

Another strange thing happened when I pulled into a parking lot in Bloomsburg. I'd had a few friends in the car. This parking lot was where a lot of people turned around in, so what I did was not unusual. All of a sudden, three or four police cars came out of nowhere, as if conducting a bust. I just looked at them and drove right through them. I had no idea what they wanted. Later on, I was to learn that someone was trying to set me up. This would come to light later on.

Most of the things that were to happen to me were brought on by my stubbornness and rebellion. One afternoon, I had gone to the car, and it wouldn't start. It was in a parking lot in Bloomsburg. I had plenty of friends around at the time, so we decided to push-start it. Tom, my brother, and Tim, my cousin, were there at the time. I climbed in the car and put it in drive, or so I thought. Everyone gave me a good push, and it started. The only problem was that it started in reverse. Tires were smoking as the car sped backward. Caught by surprise, it threw me forward, and the gas pedal stuck to the floor. Looking to the rear, all I could see was people jumping out of the way. I thought for sure I had run over Tim. Lucky for him, he was fast on his feet. The shift button was in drive at the time this had happened. That was the last for the Dodge as it made another ten miles and threw a rod bearing. I don't remember what happened to it after that.

From this time on, I was on foot. I walked everywhere I needed to go unless someone was going in that direction. Needless to say, I then lost my job, as I had no way to get there. That also meant I could no longer pay for my room above the bar. I stayed wherever I could at friends' houses. Of course, this was to be short-lived, as most of my friends lived with their parents. I had a lot to learn, and this went on for some time. I finally got tired of trying to survive this way. I was heading for trouble, and I knew it. Then I made another mistake. This one would put my life in a spin.

The Military

WALKING DOWN THE ROAD WITH a friend, I talked to him about how I was sick of this life and had to do something about it. Somehow, we got discussing the options around us. Without a vehicle to get to a job, this limited us to only one option, the military. After discussing this prospect, we decided to join the navy and have something to do with aircraft. We then went to the recruiter and took a test on different things. A little while later, the recruiter came back and said only I had passed the test. It seemed my friend had not. Oh God, I needed to get away from there so bad. I didn't want to get stuck in any place even close to Penna. I decided to go alone and get as far away as I could. The West Coast was the farthest I could get for now. I asked the recruiter to get me gone as soon as possible. Word came back that I would be gone in three days. I agreed to go at that time.

The next thing I knew, I was taking a physical and an oath in front of the flag. Then it's on to the airport and a flight to Great Lakes, Illinois. On the bus, I looked at other kids who had made the same mistake as I had. It seemed all of us didn't know what to expect. As the bus came to a stop, we were told to get off. It seemed that the language got sterner and more demanding. I had an uneasy feeling as we walked into a tunnel, headed to who knows where. As we were walking in, some people were coming out. "If you have cigarettes, smoke 'em," someone said as they passed by. Taking the clue and getting more nervous, I fired one up. As we cleared the tunnel, I knew then I'd made a serious mistake. Life as I knew it was about to take a serious turn.

As was the drill, we were given military garb and a stretch hat. We were now called raisins and treated as such. We were marched to the barber for our military haircut. Hurry and wait was the game theme at all times. Everywhere we went, we either marched or ran. We stenciled our dumb-looking uniforms and mailed our civilian clothes home. Now they had us. You can recognize a raisin a mile off by his uniform. In the morning around four, I think, someone would put their rifle in the garbage can and slam it around. I wanted to kill that sucker. There had to be a better way. Of course, the worst part was we didn't get to smoke. It wasn't long before I messed up. Sneaking a smoke in the bathroom, I was busted by the company commander. I hadn't even got a good inhale when the bathroom door opened. As quick as it was, someone must have snitched.

I learned fast on how to do lots and lots of push-ups. Then came happy hour, about three of them in a row. This consisted of a huge arena with an asphalt floor. With weapon in hand, you held it above your head and ran around and around. Some guys were passing out and were then noticed by the DIs. This is what you wouldn't want. They'd kick you and scream all the more. Push-ups on your rifle with your knuckles under it seemed to take the skin off. Getting up from the floor to run again, you'd leave a perfect body print in sweat. This went on for more than an hour, I'm sure, even though I didn't have a watch. When this was done, you gimped back to the barracks. Then you'd take a shower. Hopefully, you didn't have the duty, or you wouldn't get any sleep.

After a while, we got a cig break. What it boils down to is good monkey, bad monkey. If you pleased the company commander, you'd get a smoke; if not, bad monkey. I guess the company commander took a liking to me and put me on laundry duty. While everyone smoked and joked, I had to check all the ties on the clothesline. I'd see a plane overhead and feel as though my spirit was going with them. I then got another favor from the CC—scullery duty for a month, that is peeling some potatoes but mostly gathering and cleaning trays. God, was that gross. I worked hard and was given the captain position. Why would I want that? I had to tell the rest what to do and keep the place operating. Of course, it was my ass if something went wrong. That finally ended, thank God.

After getting back to the barracks, it didn't take long for some-one to set me up. With our racks made up and we were out march-ing, someone put a hangman's noose on my rack. It just so happened we had an inspection that day. I got back and soon I was talking to someone I didn't even know. He was telling me that it was a sign of mutiny. I told him I didn't even know how to make one. Didn't mat-ter; here's another four happy hours. As I grabbed my rifle to head to the drill arena, I yelled so all could hear. "When I find you, you won't see home again. You'll die here." I meant every word. It didn't take me long to find an easier way to deal with the grueling physical torture. If you run in the middle of the group as you run the arena, keep your gun lower, and it wasn't as heavy as you ran. The circle in the center of the arena was a smaller circle. That way, you didn't run as far. When you did push-ups on your rifle, slip your fingers slightly out from under the weapon. That way, it didn't wear the skin off your fingers. Only when the gestapo came around did you slip your fingers under the weapon. They had a lot of people to torture at the time. This went on every week for a month. My anger started to rise within me. Finally, they caught the guy who was setting everyone up. He was blowing his nose on someone's bedsheet before inspection. No one would tell me who he was though. I had a score to settle.

Not only did we march all day; I also had to deal with happy hour and the laundry detail when we got a break. Our ARPOC who was one of us but was favored by the company commander got to carry a saber. He also was the pivot point when we turned in forma-tion. One night, someone took his saber while he was sleeping and stuck him with it. I didn't hear anyone scream, but then I was dead tired at the end of the day. The next day, he was gone, but I don't know if he died or not. He just wasn't there anymore. From that time on, there was no more saber allowed. Then came graduation day. A lot of our company were happy. We marched around in front of a lot of people and headed back to the barracks. Everyone was busy and excited. It seemed their families had been there that day, and they couldn't wait to see them. I could care less about it. As I was stand-ing in the barracks, I heard the guy on guard duty ask the company commander if he could get a break to see his family. I took his place so he could see his folks. The CC was surprised to know I had no one to visit with. He looked kinda shocked.

The day came when we were to get our orders. We were all sitting on the floor as our orders were called out. They asked for volunteers for submarine duty. It's good food and good crew, they said. Something's wrong with that, I thought. A few did just that. At least I got the West Coast as I'd hoped for, USS *Ranger* CVA-61, San Francisco, California. I was also an airman and had to stay for advanced training at Great Lakes, Illinois. Oh, what fun! A few weeks later, I was on a plane headed back to Pennsylvania for furlough. Getting home didn't seem like much to me. The same thing as before, I didn't know where anyone was at the time. I did get to see my grandma; she gave me a hug and said, "There's some good in you. I know there is." Soon, I was on a plane headed to California. I got shuffled around a few places, which didn't make sense to me, but it's the government. I just happened to run into a guy who told me, "Whatever you do, stay out of the V2 division."

Arriving in San Francisco, I finally got to the ship. Looking around, it didn't look like much with all the hoses and wires running into it. It was kinda disgusting to look at, if you ask me. Getting up where I belonged took a little doing. We grouped together in a room and were told which divisions we were to be in. Of course, I ended up in the V2 division, catapult number 1. Boy, did I luck out… yeah right! Then the news came someone had died in my family. Getting down to the pay phone on the dock, I called home and heard Grandma had died. She had a blood clot that went from her arm to her lungs. All I could do was stand there and cry. I loved her. She was filled with the Spirit. Righteous, not religious. She was so full of peace. I still miss her today. When I got back to the division, they could see I had been sobbing. It was too late to see her off as too much time had passed.

Life on the ship was kinda hard to take. Being the new guy, you got all the fire watches. This consisted of standing in one place with a fire extinguisher while someone welded on the ship. You stood on a pad of insulation, which I'm sure was asbestos. What was going to catch fire anyway? It was all metal. Smoke filled the place and made me want to puke. Another fun activity was hanging over the side with a needle gun, chipping off the paint. The place was full of noise, with a lot of hoses to step over. Somehow, I got picked to operate the retraction engine just below deck. The guy who trained me was a colored guy named J.T. We got to know each other pretty well. To this day, I still consider him a brother. Anyway, the RT, as it was called, pulled the shuttle back after an airplane was launched. There were a lot of hydraulics and steam pipes that protruded into the console area. The RT also had two huge hydraulic pumps that just screamed when in use. To make matters worse, there were cables and a crosshead with pulleys that ran back and forth with each shot. Grease flew everywhere. It was my job to use solvent and rags to clean it up. The day finally came when we were to pull out of dry dock.

Of course, all that time in dry dock, we did get liberty (time off) to go into town. I wasn't ready for all the cons and scams. I usually walked alone, and to this day, I'm not sure why. I guess I didn't really trust anyone. Oakland and San Francisco were quite different than what I had been used to in Pennsylvania. Sex was plastered on the business signs all over the streets. Hookers tried to sell you their wares. Cons were everywhere, selling anything from sex to drugs. Not only that, but they hated us for being military. There had been killings of a few veterans in San Francisco. I didn't know them personally, thank God. It seemed they had been shot execution style. We were told to run in groups for protection. The hate grew between us. Meeting a friend on board, we got to talking about parachuting. He'd done it before. I thought it sounded good. The next thing I knew, I was up in a plane over Chula Vista, California. I bowed my head and thought, *Lord, my life is in your hands.* Leaving the plane was great; all went well. It was a rush like I had never had in my entire life. I was on a static line as I was told I wouldn't know when to pull the cord. I almost hit the circle on the ground. The instructor asked me if I'd jumped before because he didn't have to tell me twice to jump. Six months later, we pulled out to sea.

Being out to sea at first seemed to be better than dry dock. Later on, you couldn't wait to get back to port. The hours were very long and exhausting. We were doing what they call carrier quals. We'd launch aircraft off, and they would fly around a little and then land on board. As they had been fueled up, we launched them again. I could hear on the communication system, which I'll call the com from here out, that the jets were dumping fuel out as soon as they were launched. This seemed odd as they were lined up at the gas stations in California. When I got the chance, I went up to the flight deck to see for myself, and sure enough, they were.

Back in port, a few of our people had rented an apartment. I usually walked alone, but I thought for once, I'd stop in and see the place. It turned out some of our people were using the needle and scag, which is street heroin. I didn't like stopping there for long, as they would ask you to try it. It didn't look like much fun to me, as they would throw up and then go to sleep. I continued to walk alone for about the entire first year, I'd say. The ship went overseas, on a WESTPAC cruise. We went to Hawaii, Philippines, and Hong Kong. This was in the years 1974 and 1975. I remember because of the jackets some people bought with the map and the year on them. After we returned to San Francisco, it was the same old thing. The people (civilians) hated us. I was wishing I was back overseas.

Then one day, as I was walking down the street, a guy named Kenny pulled over in his sports car and asked me if I wanted to ride in the mountains. He was from catapult number 2. It sure sounded like fun. As we went up the mountains, we met Danny. He also had a sports car. Before you knew it, I was riding with him. Around the mountains, we go racing. This was cool; we're in the lead. Danny looked over his shoulder to see how far ahead we were. There was a car coming at us. He turned around just in time to turn the wheel. Down the one-way street we went. As more cars were coming, he turned to cross the median, only it was not there anymore. It had been dug out by construction. "Pow!" He blew all his tires and ruined his rims. So much for racing! I got to really liking these guys. They were nuts. From then on, I started running with them. This is when all the trouble started, for me anyway.

We were out to sea, and we were launching around the clock. The LT who had just taken over command of bow cats, as we were called, was a real winner. I'll leave him nameless as he knows who he is. The place was coming apart as the vibration was shaking the pipes terribly. I was putting buckets around to catch the hydraulics. Lucky for me, no pipes blew apart, or I would have been killed as the pressure was 2,750 psi. At that pressure, it would cut you, and you would not heal from the hydraulics. We somehow got a break but not long enough to get any sleep. We then asked the LT if he could possibly get us reliefs from the aft cats, as they couldn't launch when jets were landing. "We'll run our own damn machines," was his reply as he walked out. It didn't take long for one of our men to make a mistake. Dave was running the console. He held our lives in his hands. He hadn't gotten but an hour of sleep. The console was steam operated and also hydraulic controlled. It set the catapult in launch position. We were doing no-loads at the time. No-loads are a practice rounds for the catapult operations. We did this to test the system before launching. The catapult went off prematurely and dragged some of my friends down the track. This was bound to happen as we were all tired to the bone. Lucky for us, it happened on a no-load, or my friends would surely have been killed. The com was buzzing with yelling as they were dragged down the track. This was enough. I then made a mistake I would pay for, for the duration of my time in the service. I picked up the phone and called the captain's hotline. When I told them what had happened, they didn't quite believe me at first. "Are you up in the tower?" I asked. "Did you see a commotion on cat number 1? I needed one man relieved from his station." Sometime later, the whole aft cat crews ran in to relieve us. We all fell to the steel floor and slept. The hydraulic motors were screaming, but we were so tired we didn't hear them at all. It seemed like only a minute, and a friend woke me up. "They think I called the captain" was his wake-up call. I couldn't let him take the fall for something I did. I walked back to the officer's compartment. I could hear them very excited and talking together. Not knowing what to say, the first words out of my mouth were, "I hear you're looking for the one who called the captain. You're looking at him." Oh boy, I had several LTs yelling at me at once. Of course, from past experience with the old man, I started yelling back. I think I started heading for the LT who had caused it from the start.

Somehow, one LT got me out to the hallway, yelling for me to calm down. I started calming down as he talked calmly to me. Then I went back to the cat. From what I heard, they hadn't seen anything like that since World War II. I don't even know what had happened.

From then on, my life got real stressful. The higher-ups were then out to get me any way they could. I knew if I ended up in the brig, I'd probably revolt to the torture they imposed on whoever was sent there. The brig was run by marines, who just hated us. Of course, the men in our cats, who had been in the brig, just hated them as bad. We were the green shirts, those who went under the jets to hook them up for launching. The flight deck was a very dangerous place. A lot was going on, and if you make a mistake, you might just die for it. Those of us who smoked pot never did so and went up to the flight deck. You'd panic and run. This was one thing you never did. A lot of us did take speed to stay alert and alive, as the days were very long and hard. I thought about those who had gotten into scag. Where did they get it when we were out to sea? They couldn't even go home on liberty and get too far from their source.

I picked up a book called UCMJ simple terms. It is the Uniform Code Military Justice broken down in layman's terms. I studied this book from cover to cover, as I needed to protect myself from being set up by my superiors. Given an order, I'd need a witness to the order, so as not to be AWOL. Any time we had a stand-down in port, I'd get special duties, KP and the like. I just kept hanging in there. The stress finally gave me an ulcer.

I finally got out of the R&T (Retraction Engine) and got on the flight deck. I did hookup and holdback on jets of different types. We had a mail plane, which everyone hated but didn't talk about. It was small and had props, which, of course, were running when you went to hook them up. They said, "Don't look at the props spinning. It will cause you to go in a trance." How do you hook up the cable on it without looking? What did I do? I looked. Sure enough, I started to walk right into the props. The only thing that stopped me was a scream from inside of me to *stop*. That voice would save me again in the future. Anyway, every time that plane rolled up, I'd curse it and go numb inside, like I was hollow. Later on, I was put on center deck.

There, I'd set the steam with the console down below. I'd operate two catapults. There was an LT right behind me, as I was communication central to the cats. He'd also cover my butt to keep me safe. One day, he gave me the order to open the center deck. As we walked out to it, we were caught in a jet blast. This sent us flying all the way up the catapult. As I looked, I thought, *We're dead. There's no more ship left, but ten feet.* As God would have it, I caught one foot on deck and threw all my weight into the LT, who was hanging onto me, as we flew down the cat. We fell in a heap. I started laughing so hard I couldn't stop. On the way back, it seemed as though we'd never get there. It seemed in slow motion or something. I don't remember opening the center deck, but I must have. I was sitting there and started laughing again uncontrollably. Danny ran out from the catwalk and started shaking me. I finally came around again and did my job. The LT must have thought I was nuts.

This same LT was jumping up and down, as we could not get any steam up to launch our jets. We had a Russian bomber coming in and were defenseless. Another carrier about five hundred miles away sent F-4s to cover us. It was always dangerous on the flight deck, with jets landing and taking off.

* * * * *

I always said what I believed and had told the crew about the farmhouse being haunted. It was because of that I was approached by one of our crewmen who I'll leave nameless as I think this is best for all. This crewman told me when he was a teenager or whatever, a friend told him there was a book in a cave, which was written in Latin. They went up there and took a chair along to sit on. He was told if anything happened to throw the book down, and it would stop. As he was reading the book, his chair started to rise with him in it. He didn't say how far it rose off the ground, but that he'd thrown the book and it stopped. It must have been high enough to scare him. That would have been the end of the story, but something happened around three to four months later as I had been on watch till four in the morning. I was coming into the sleeping quarters. I was very tired, and for once in my life, my mind was blank. As I neared his bed, a laugh came from it that was so hideous and filled with hate it made my hair stand up in the back. It hadn't been him, as no human could voice something like that nor record it either. I pulled back out of the sleeping area, shaking like a little child. I tried to drink a cup of coffee but kept spilling it. I gave up on the coffee and slid back into the sleeping area, staying as far from him as I could. I then slid into bed and pulled the covers over my head and shook myself to sleep. In the morning, I told him what had happened. He got very depressed and quiet. I knew he hadn't done it. A lot of these self-help books tell you to meditate and let your mind go blank. Don't do it. It's a way to let the evil in. It took eight years after the service to get over what had happened there. I'd look around while I was in the bars and think to myself, *If you only knew, you wouldn't be laughing.*

The day came when I found a motorcycle in the paper. I took a friend named Kenny to go look at it. It was a Honda 750 with some neat exhaust pipes on it. It was colored blue and had lots of chrome. We took it for a ride, and I loved it. I bought it that day and took it to base. It gave me a great morale boost, as I could get away from the navy towns where it seemed everyone hated us. The ship changed ports to San Diego, California. I loaded the bike on the ship in the hangar bay. Things got better down there, as there were more places to go with the bike although the people there also didn't care for us. Kenny wanted to see his girlfriend up in Salt Lake City. We decided to go up there on the bike. All went well until we got to Nevada. It was November, and it started to get cold, and finally, we got to the snow, two inches to be exact. Kenny was in love and really wanted to see his woman. We continued on in the snow and hail. When we got to the hail, I let Kenny drive. After all, it was his idea. It was like riding into buckshot; it sure did hurt. We finally made it to SLC. I decided to leave the bike and fly back.

Upon arrival back to the ship, things went as usual. Launch jets while at sea and try to cover my back from the higher-ups. It seemed they all wanted a piece of me, as my time was getting shorter to get out. The day came when I got called to the officer's coop. LT asked me, "When are you going to take your third class test?" I had already done so and passed it. Of course, he wanted me to do it again. I knew I was too short in time to get an upgrade. Telling him that, he reached in his drawer and pulled out some report chits. Oh no, here I go again, back to captain's mast. I stood out on the flight deck the night before captain's mast. It was cold out, and I had a blanket wrapped around me. I was just thinking, so close and yet so far. Almost out and now I'll be in the brig and probably revolt and get sent to Leavenworth (military prison). Standing in line with around fifteen others, I was just bumming while the others seemed to be joking around. As I was standing in front of the captain, he asked me, "What is your problem?" I didn't know what else to say except, "Well, sir, I use drugs, meaning pot, and sometimes speed (oral)." I sure couldn't try to explain that I'm being set up. He probably wouldn't believe that. The captain dismissed all the charges. All I could do was stand there in disbelief. Finally, it dawned on me that I wasn't going to the brig, and I saluted and started walking out. Before I got to the door, I got another report chit for my hair being too long. I must have really aged while I was standing there. I went down and got my hair cut really short and was okay to go.

Time went on, and it's back to sea again. It was almost the holidays, and the ship pulled in for a stand-down. A stand-down is a vacation for the majority of the crew. Of course, this time I got orders to report to Nas Miramar, right before the holidays and, of course, at my twenty-first birthday. Nas Miramar is a naval station in California for rehabilitation. We had a good party before I left my friends. They took me up and dropped me off at Nas Miramar.

"We got one," was their reply as I stepped in. I was two sheets to the wind. After being searched, I was shown to my bunk. The next day was quite different from my usual. It seemed there were two groups of people, the introverts and the extroverts. It was what they called group therapy. At first, they put me in the introvert group. I wouldn't say anything, as I was trying to figure it all out. All I knew was the lady leading the group was into witchcraft. I didn't want any part of that. They then put me in the other group. The lady, Mari, who led that group, really didn't like me. I was then put under some guy who did repairs and maintenance on the buildings. All he could talk about was killing gooks. I liked him a lot. Whatever he said to do, I did. I was hanging out the windows, enjoying the sunshine and cleaning windows. I guess I must have liked it too much. They noticed and pulled me off the maintenance crew. Now I was back in group therapy again. I shouldn't have been smiling, I guess. Things changed when I asked a person in charge what my chances were of getting an honorable discharge out of the place. I watched him run right over to Mari and tell her. From then on, her attitude toward me changed. I spent my birthday staring at the ceiling as we were confined to a certain level in the building. Later as they got to trust you, liberty was given.

I then started to talk in the group more. I told them of what had happened on the *Ranger* and about making the LTs look bad. Mari told me one day, "Get your GED here, and I'll let you out of the military." I really hit the books. I studied so hard I'd get a headache.

Mari asked, "How did you stand the military so long?" I replied, "Just getting high was how I coped with it." The day came when I was released from the service. I was so happy I threw all my uniforms in the trash, except my bell-bottoms and a peacoat. I walked off the base. I didn't even call a cab. It was as though the chains fell off as I walked off the base. I stuck my thumb out and had a ride in just a few minutes. I went down to a friend's house; he had gotten out also. We had a good party, and then he took me to the airport. I caught a flight to Salt Lake City to get my bike.

The Road

Once I got to SLC, a friend picked me up. His name was Rick. He had also been on the catapult crew. Rick took me over to get my bike at Ken's woman's place. It had been stored in their garage. It looked in good shape. The only thing I hadn't checked were the most important, the tires. As Rick took off, I hit the gas to catch up to him. He was disappearing over a knoll in the road. No sooner had I reached the top of the knoll than my rear tire blew out. I'd been doing 60 mph at the time, and it turned my bike sideways as I was sliding down the road. I kept the bike up as it slid down the road with traffic right behind me. I'm not sure how far I slid, but I was white as a ghost, Rick commented. People driving by were giving me thumbs up as they passed by. I wouldn't leave the bike, so Rick went and got help. We took it to a friend of Rick's and put it under their carport. After we got it fixed, I then started to get in trouble by driving around town. It seemed they had a law, no helmet under 35 mph, but over that, one was required. After being pulled over once, and my bike being almost towed, I then started to outrun the police when the lights came on. It didn't happen too often, as I was pretty lucky. My tags were about to run out, so I decided to go to California and got new ones. I could have probably used the mail, but I wanted to go cross-country on my bike. Starting from Utah just wouldn't do it.

I'd talked about it when I was in the military. I strapped my green military bag on the rear bar so I could lie back on it. I already had cruise pegs on the bike, so I could relax as I drove. It was early March when I left SLC for California. It was pretty cool, but it got warmed up as I got nearer to California. I ended up in some little town and got my tags. I then started back toward Utah. I came to a fork in the road on the way back. One direction would take me to see Kenny, but I thought about how I would never walk through a military checkpoint again, as he was on a military base. I just couldn't do it. As I drove through Nevada. I stopped to look at a bunch of pine trees. They had been frosted to the point of looking like crystals. I was to see a lot more in the years to come.

I finally rolled back into SLC. I then got to a phone and called my friend Rick. I had one question for him: Did he want to split a place here in SLC? Getting his answer, I then decided to head across to Pennsylvania. Rick had it made as he was in a cool place with a lot of people around, mostly kids. I had no problem with his decision, but I knew without a job, my funds would run out in a while. The decision to hit the road was a logical one even though it was pretty cold. Heading up the freeway, I stopped and looked at the mountains surrounding SLC. I took one final look back down the valley, then it was full bore down I-80, eastbound. Getting to Evanston, Wyoming, took very little time, and I just fueled up and took off again. It seemed eventless as I drove on. When I got to a place called Elk Mountain, it got very, very cold. My knees were knocking as I drove down the road. I finally got over it, and things warmed up a bit, but not much. I remember driving into some little place where I pulled in to get some fuel, as I didn't know when I'd be able to fuel up down the road. The lady at the register told me I'd just missed it. It seemed a guy had wrapped his kid in the barbed wire fence just down the road and shot him to death. I looked up the road at the fence and got a queasy gut feeling. Had I'd been there, I would have probably shot the guy, as I was also packing a firearm.

Leaving there seemed a load off my mind. I was glad I missed that. As I was heading into Nebraska, it still seemed quite cool to be on a bike. The mountains seemed to fade away into foothills. I still had to deal with the rain though. I don't remember where, but the rain got so bad I stopped to get a room. It was way overpriced and didn't even have a TV to watch. I dried my clothes the best I could and got a little sleep. I dried off the pistol and wiped off all the ammo. If I needed to use it, I wouldn't have time to find the shell casings. I was glad to leave there and get down the road again. I felt in control when I rode, as I could go where I pleased.

Rolling into Iowa was nice, as it was warmer, and it felt good as I drove over the knolls. The people seemed real friendly, and the food was great. When I got to the eastern part of the state, I drove through a bunch of bugs, which were hanging out on the road. I was covered from head to toe with dead bugs. The bike didn't do much better. Getting to Illinois, I started to get low on money. I called Ma, and she wired me some money through Western Union. The only trouble was I had to go downtown to get it. I found it all right and drove down the sidewalk to the Western Union. As I passed by, two people commented on me using the sidewalk. I couldn't blame them, but I wasn't going to let anyone get near the bike. I parked on the sidewalk out in front of the place. On the road again, I found the road seemed rougher and had more potholes to miss. Once I got to Indiana, the road was smooth, as it was a toll road, all the way to Ohio. Ohio was a little stressful, as the traffic got worse, and the potholes seemed to continue forever.

It was late in the evening when I reached the Pennsylvania border. I yelled as I crossed the state line, "I'd made it!" I was very tired and sore, but I drove on. I didn't know what to expect when I got home. I wasn't very excited about getting there. It seemed too many memories were coming back, and they weren't good ones. I didn't know it at the time, but I'd need the road again. It was a tough road, but it helped you forget.

I got my hands on a Ford van. It was rough-looking, and the leaf springs stuck up in the back, through the floor. My brother Tom helped me bolt bulldozer track to the floor of the van. This stopped the springs from coming through. Tom started painting the van with gold metallic paint. It was starting to look good as he was putting on the last coat. Pa, for whatever reason, started the hay baler and started coming down from the barn with it. He had it running as he drove down toward the shed where Tom was painting the van. Of course, this got dust flying around, which was sticking to the paint. I was very angry because he was doing this on purpose. Pa was acting jealous because the van was looking too good. I grabbed the .22 rifle and was going to shoot off the lens next to Pa. My brother grabbed the rifle out of my hands. "I'm not gonna shoot 'im," I said, "just the lens." Of course, the dust had the desired effect and stuck to the paint. I was not to be the only one to aim a rifle at Pa. My brother did the same thing but aimed at his head. This happened later on when I wasn't there.

We fixed the van up inside with carpet and a bed. Later on, my brother and I took off, heading to Alaska. I don't know where we had acquired the money, and I don't think we had enough at the time. Tom had a bad time driving and would get bored of the road and head out on dirt roads that ran along the interstate. Of course, I'd wake up to find that we were lost someplace. We ran into a road-block. They were checking vehicles for anything out of the ordinary. Even though I had my license in the glove box, I told them I didn't have it with me because I didn't want to open the glove box and get shot because I had a gun in there. We had my bike strapped in the van. I guess it wasn't good enough. The bike fell over, and the gas tank got crushed. I didn't know what had happened or where he had been driving. I woke up to the damaged bike. It made me sick to look at it. We sold it in Salt Lake City real cheap. This gave us the money to try for Alaska. We got to the Canadian border, and they wouldn't let us through. It seemed they thought we'd try to stay in Canada to work. Of course, this was all my brother could stand and wanted to go home. I got him a plane ticket, and he flew home.

I had all our belongings in the van as I headed east. I picked up two hitchhikers on the way. Driving through a lightning storm out in the plains was breathtaking. I couldn't figure how we had got-ten through without being struck. The sides of the van shook as the lightning hit all around us. It just so happened one of the hitchhikers stole my brother's gun when I wasn't looking. It really bummed me out. Getting back to Pennsylvania, we called the police, which was in the state where the hitchhiker had gotten off. They picked him up really quickly. We didn't press charges, and he was released soon after.

It just so happened I met a woman in Pennsylvania who I'll call Amy. I was in more fights that year with people because of her than I have been in since, most of them Amy started. She would walk up to someone and instigate a fight. I don't know why, but I fell in love with her, and soon we were living together. I would have nightmares about my times in the service and wake up in a heavy sweat. Amy would change the sheets on the bed.

We went through three vehicles that year. Some got tore up; others we had to sell in need of money. We ended up in a home where they rented us a room. The only way we could use food stamps was to get food you had to cook. We had a hot plate, which we used. This also got us in trouble with the homeowner. Amy happened to get pregnant and decided to abort it. At first, this didn't bother me, but the closer it got, the more I couldn't stand it. I tried to stop her from doing the abortion. One of her family members helped her get it done; I can't remember who. She came back and said the nurses had said, "Oh my god. It might have been twins." I left her as my love turned cold. I just couldn't be with her anymore after she did the abortion. The vehicle we had at that time was an old truck, which she took, as it was in her name. We did it that way because the insurance was cheaper for a female than a male at the time.

I ended up staying at my brother's house that just so happened to be a place that Amy and I had rented before. I had nowhere to go but there. My nerves were shot, and I couldn't feel hot or cold water. I almost cut my throat while shaving. I threw the razor and ran downstairs. I finally went to the local doctor, and he put me on some medication for nerves. It seemed to do the trick. As time went on, I moved in with my cousin.

A lot of times, I worked at a horse ranch. I started out on the ground crew and then started working with the horses. I enjoyed that. The only problem was that the pay was low, and the rent was high, it being a college town. I would usually work two jobs and save up money to leave the state. It seemed there was no hope for a decent-paying job. Most places that had a future only hired minorities, as they got government funds for doing so. Somewhere in between this period of time, my uncle Kenny had a massive heart attack. We went to the hospital to see him. As we went, I prayed and asked God to give him my heart. I didn't even know God at this point in my life. Why would he answer me, of all people? God did heal Kenny. The doctor was amazed. He stated he had a heart of a twenty-one-year-old! Kenny went home soon after. He never had heart trouble after that either.

I left for Utah, as I had friends there, and the pay was better than Pennsylvania. I worked in concrete for a few years, and then the bottom fell out of the housing boom. In Utah, I met a lady friend who tried to help me as I was very negative and angry. She would take me up the mountains at my request and drop me off. I'd camp out and sit by the river or up on a cliff. I had a lot to think about and to sort out. Now that I think back, God must have put her in my life at just the right time. It was usually for three days at a time.

I returned to Pennsylvania and did the same thing, working two jobs to get enough money to get out. I went to Colorado looking for a way into the Forest Service. I knew civil service had good pay and benefits. While I was looking, I got information about a maintenance job for the government at Tooele Army Depot. I went over to Utah, as it was close to Colorado, and put an application in. I saw some friends and headed back to Colorado. It wasn't long, and I got a job there. I returned to Utah and worked till I was laid off at Tooele. It seemed the job was temporary. Then it was back to construction again with its ups and downs. I'd get laid off and head down the road again. I'd go visit the family for a couple months and get money up to head down the road again. As long as the lines on the road kept passing me by, I felt good. I should have gotten into trucking long haul, but without experience, no one would hire you. It was to happen in later years, though only for a few years.

My anger grew as each day went by. It was getting to be a lot more than I could handle. It seemed to eat at my insides. When I felt angry, I would hunt for someone to piss me off. It always seemed when I looked, I couldn't find the person to take my anger out on. God must have kept me from the fight. It seemed nothing I would do in life worked out. I was fed up with it all. My friend Tom and I would look for places to rent, which looked like they needed a little work, because we didn't have money for the deposit and first and last month's rent. Our plan was to work off the deposit. We passed by a house that looked promising. Stopping by, we were surprised to find the doors open. I didn't know it at the time, but this house was to be a life changer.

I'll let the address be unknown as the owner might be offended, even though it is burned in my mind forever. It was a two-story house, which was older and needed some work. It didn't take too long to find the owner, and to our surprise, we didn't need a deposit. He seemed eager to rent the place. Tom and his woman took the downstairs, and I took the upper rooms. My part had a larger bedroom and a small room that led to a stairway on the outside of the house. The stairway didn't look safe, so I didn't use it. I just locked the door to the steps. I had a set of beads that I put across the doorway to the bedroom. It was kinda like in the sixties when they had beads for the door. To my surprise, three strands in the middle of my door beads would swing just a little all the time. I tried to find a draft but couldn't. It didn't take long, and things started to bang around downstairs at night. I asked Tom, "What were you building down here?" Nothing was the answer. He'd also hear me upstairs even when I wasn't there. We were told by some people that the place was haunted. By then, we already knew. One day, a guy stopped by and said, "Talk to her, and she'll stop banging around." He wouldn't come in the house though. This is just what I did. I wanted to help her somehow. Talk about the blind leading the blind. As I was walking up the stairway to my room, I felt her walk right through me. It almost took my breath away. It wasn't the evil I had felt at the farm, but I didn't know what to make of it.

Work had been hard to find. I had been working for a small concrete company. There was only three of us, the boss and another finisher. I was the laborer, of course. The major problem was every payday, I received only some of my pay. As I lived hand to mouth, it didn't take long for me to run out of money and food. After three days, I was so weak I couldn't even swing the hammer to drive stakes. I quit that day and went home. Sitting in my room that night, I thought, *What a world. We'd killed the only one who truly loved us. Jesus Christ, forgive me.* All of a sudden, it felt as though the whole world was taken from my shoulders. I was on my knees and just cried and cried. I lost track of time.

The next morning, my housemates downstairs knew something had happened that night. I don't know if they heard me or what. Not only that, but the spirit that had been there all that time was gone. Hopefully, it went home with Jesus. I've been by the place since, and people live there, so it must be okay. It wasn't long after that I ended up on the street for a month. I had a truck but no gas, so at least I had a place to sleep. I also had a kerosene stove and kerosene for it. As I was sitting on the curb, I noticed someone coming up the street. He was carrying a box on his shoulder. When he got closer, I knew who it was. We had let him stay with us for a while at another place. He had a box of Top Ramen, a whole case. "This is for you," he said.

"How did you know I didn't have any food?" I asked.

"I had a feeling," he said.

God did provide, just as he said he would. I couldn't stop smiling and was well fed for a month.

I got a hold of some money and started heading back to Pennsylvania. Somewhere in Wyoming, I got a flat tire. Not only that, but the truck was using too much gas for the funds I had acquired. I called my brother Tom, and he agreed to buy my truck unseen. He sent some money by Western Union. That gave me enough money to make it back. It didn't take long, and I fell from believing that I had been saved. I should have picked up a Bible, read it, and got with other believers. This is very important, as the enemy is as a roaming lion who picks off the strays. There is strength in numbers.

There was a neighbor who had the farm above ours. Her name was Elisie. Quite often, I would work for her when I came in from the road. She was a shining light to me. On the road, you couldn't trust anyone. Elisie would never lie. It was refreshing to me.

Years went by, and I ended up in Utah again. I finished my GED and had some technical college in diesel mechanics. I was debating going to a trucking school, as now they trained people on the job. I received a letter from the government to test for a job as an aircraft mechanic. I passed the first test and took four weeks of college to prepare for the interview. Passing that, I was hired and started working on F-4s. We had college one week a month for aircraft tech. I really liked this job, but within two years, a group of us were laid off. I moved to Montana with my girlfriend. She was from Butte, Montana. Our relationship didn't last because I wasn't working, and she was seeing other people. I went back to Pennsylvania, but I missed being around her little boy, Rusty. I went back to Montana and ended up in Seeley Lake. It was here that I started driving long haul. I went from pulling reefers to dry vans and finally flatbeds. I had about two and a half years in, and I injured my back in Texas. I was relocating tarps and the spare tire when it happened. The next mistake I made was driving into Montana on a back injury. I knew I was hurt bad, but I tried to go back to work. That didn't help anything at all.

Now I was to learn about workman's comp. They send you to doctors who will give them the report they desire, no matter what the truth is. To add insult to injury, they tell you it's all in your head. I was living with Angie at the time, and I thank God for her as she helped me through the rough times. Finally, she talked me into going to the VA hospital. There they took a CT scan and found a serious problem. I had fractured a disc in my lower back, and another one had pushed up into my vertebrae and compressing my spinal cord. Without an operation, I would be crippled. One year later, they called me down to Utah for the operation. It had been three years since the injury. It's taken fifteen years to get this good. I still use a walking stick quite often when my back is hurting. I don't pass out anymore and seem to have my legs back. Don't these doctors know they must be judged for what they do? Be warned, for God knows all things!

The injury took me off the road and brought me back to God. I had a trail to walk every day, which took me through a bird sanctuary and along the river. I lived outside of Seeley Lake, Montana. As I viewed all of God's beauty, I would kneel down and pray to thank him for all he's given us.

Then one night, I had a vivid dream of people waving for me to come to them. I didn't know what to make of it at first. The next night, I had the same dream. I knew then what God was telling me. He wanted me to go to church. Not only that, but I had to get up in front of the congregation to tell them of my grandmother and what she had told me. It felt as though my chest would explode if I didn't. This is my greatest fear. To speak in front of a crowd. I then got a burning desire to know more about Jesus. I showed up at the Bible studies. This is what I should have done the first time God had called me. The pastor then baptized me at my request. That set off a chain of events.

We had a wood stove at home. It was getting near fall, and we had the fire going. All of a sudden, the temperature dropped about twenty degrees. Black birds were trying to get to warmth wherever they could. A bird dropped down the stove pipe and was clawing inside the pipe. Angie had walked outside and heard the birds squawking. She came inside and started to cry because of the birds. I pulled the stove out and took the pipe apart and shook the bird out. It looked dead. Holding it, I walked outside, asking the Lord, "Please don't let this be in vain." I blew in the bird's face, but it didn't help. I stood there with the bird in my hands. All of a sudden, it came around and flew to a tree very close by and started to sing. I didn't even know they could do that. Of course, I had to get a neighbor to help me put the stove back together, as it was very heavy.

The next day, when I took my walk around the river, I was thinking of my uncle Jim and if he had made it to heaven. He had drunk himself to death after his wife died. It was a clear blue sky that day, and a small wisp of clouds started to form a name. It looked like Tim at first but changed to Jim. I thought, oh that's nice, and kept walking down the trail. Something kept bugging me though. The *i* was dotted. Hey, the *i* was dotted! Oh, now I got it. I'm a slow learner, I guess. Jim did make it to heaven and is with grandma.

As I kept walking, I was also thinking of what the pastor had said when I asked him what God wanted with me. He was reading the Bible and discussing the two witnesses. I thought, *Wow, these guys are after the rapture, aren't they?* I got to thinking, *Lord how would I know I had not failed you?* The word *come* appeared in the sky. I was blown away by that. This is why I must witness to you now. We are all God's witnesses. We're in the final days.

People in the church were having dreams and telling about them. The church was packed with people. Not only our church but many churches in the area. In Joel, it talks of God pouring out his Spirit before the end days. Joel 2:28 states, "And it shall come to pass afterward, that I will pour out my spirit upon all flesh, and your sons and your daughters shall prophesy. Your old men shall dream dreams, your young men shall see visions."

I had another vision during that time. My son, Rusty, and I were working on Angie's car out back of the house. As I looked to the left, I could see a person walking in a robe of some kind. It was an off-white color. What got me was that he was walking in his bare feet. There were a lot of thistles out back. I was thinking, *That's got to be hard on the feet.* I could see him from the waist down, as I was looking at his feet. Then he was gone. I didn't know what to make of the whole situation.

Months later, a lady named Linda Lanier came to our church. She travels around the states and sings for churches. During the sermon, she stated that someone in the church had seen an angel. I didn't know what to say, as I didn't even have it straight in my own mind. I didn't stand up or raise my hand in recognition. Later on, when she came to church again, I told her what had happened. She said that sometimes you have to step outside of your comfort zone. I felt sorry for not standing up the first time.

I had another vivid dream. Clouds were flying by me, as though I were flying through them. Up ahead, I saw Jesus and I standing in a clearing. All of a sudden, I was in me, looking at him. I looked down at his feet. He had a white robe on and sandals on his feet. As I looked up, all I could think of was "I love you." Jesus motioned to some crosses on a rack, which extended into the clouds as we were in a clearing. "Will you pick up your cross and follow me?" he asked.

"Yes," I said.

He grabbed a cross and started walking away. I did the same and turned to follow. Jesus was disappearing into the clouds. I started running as fast as I could. All I could see of him were the sandals as he walked. I didn't care what was in the clouds as long as I could catch up to him. This is where the dream stopped.

It wasn't long after that, that I told Angie I was going to put a cross on the property, right in front of the house. She didn't know what to think about that. I assembled it out of 2 x 4s and cemented it into the ground. I thought I might paint it brown to match the house. When I went to the store, I ran into a whole pile of paint cans. They were all white and on sale. *God must want it white*, I thought. I painted it white. Later on, folks would use it as a land marker to give people directions.

The day came when I heard about a friend down in Salt Lake City who had liver cancer. He'd been to the VA hospital, and they hadn't told him much. I'd known from my neighbor that when you have cancer in your liver, there's no chance of getting a transplant. I decided to travel down to Utah to see Ray and tell him of Jesus. On the way down as I was driving, it felt as though a little child was sitting in the back of the vehicle and hugging my neck with their arms around me. It was comforting and felt like I was doing what I was supposed to be doing. When I got there, I stopped at a friend's house. Ray came over there, and we talked for a while. Ray was living in a camper, as he'd sold his house. I asked Ray if I could stay over at his place. He thought it was a bad idea, as something was telling him to kill people. I'd come all that way to talk to him, so I insisted.

After getting over to his camper, we talked a little more. I just mentioned the name of Jesus, and I saw something peel off his back and fly up to the corner of his camper. It looked like a piece of carpet with a little chicken head on it. *I must have been driving too long*, I thought. Just then, another one flew off. This one had a white head. They were in the corner and looked scared. I knew then what these were. "In the name of Jesus Christ, be gone from here," I said. They disappeared. Ray had just walked up to the kitchen of the camper and looked at me funny. I didn't say anything about it at that time. It was getting late, so we went to sleep. The next day, I still didn't say any more about what I'd seen or of what I knew of his liver problem. It seemed Ray really didn't want me to stay over there again, so I decided to head back to Montana. On the way back, I realized I hadn't told Ray how to protect himself from the demons I'd seen. I called him on the phone and told him not to take the phone from his ear. Again, I spoke the name of Jesus and told the demons to leave. I then told Ray to use those words if they should bother him again. I saw Ray and his brother about a year later. Ray was not bothered with the hatred anymore. Later on, I put together a letter that explained the things I'd encountered in my life pertaining to the spiritual events I'd seen. I had hoped Ray would come to know Jesus. He died a few years later.

* * * * *

A lady named Fran Lance came to our church. She was well known and had the gift of prophecy. The church was packed the day she arrived there. They had set up a table and also a cassette recorder to record the personal prophecies. Fran would record the sitting and give God's prophecy to the person. It was always personal, and they also received a verse from the Bible. Angie was with me at the time, and we were the second persons in line to have our verses told. As Fran started talking to us, I heard a male voice from behind saying, "You're late." I wanted to crawl under the chair. It must have touched God's heart because Fran started to say, "Ooh, but look at the compassion you've learned." God also said to me, "I know you really don't like people, and you would like to go up the mountains alone and go fishing." This is what I had planned for a decade. I could see where this world was heading and didn't want any part of it. "There is something you need to do. These people need miracles to believe," he said. From that day on, I put my plan away of heading to the mountains to avoid the new world order.

Later on, I felt as though I needed to tell my family that God was returning very soon. I decided to drive to Pennsylvania where my family all live. Before I left, the pastor informed me to expect resistance. As I was driving in North Dakota, a star was so bright I pulled over twice to try and get a picture of it. They never came out when I got the film developed. I pulled off the freeway to fuel up. Trying to get into the gas station, I was blocked by construction. I went down the road a little further, and it looked as though the road stopped. Taking a left turn, I somehow ended up in a church parking lot. I got out of the car to get a better view of how to get out of the parking lot. As I looked up, I noticed the star was now dim. I was looking in the same direction as when it was bright, thinking God must want me to see something here. I slept in the car for about three hours. When nothing happened, I looked at the church sign. There were Sunday and Wednesday services. For some reason, I chose to stop back in a week on Wednesday. I needed to see what God had in store. On my way back, I found a way into the gas station to get fuel and coffee. I continued on to Pennsylvania.

Once I got to Catawissa, Pennsylvania, I decided to stay over at my brother's place. Tom had a small camper out back, and it was very comfortable. Ma gave me some pop to drink while I was there. The camper had electric hooked up to it by an extension cord. It also had propane, so I could make coffee in the mornings. Tom and Debbie, his daughter, were out back, and I started to tell them about why I thought this world was soon to come to an end. To me, all the signs spoken of in the Bible had come to pass, with a few exceptions. There had been a lot of strange weather events around the world, also whales and dolphins washing up on shore. As I was telling them about different things, I took a swig of pop from the can I had opened the night before. It seemed like a bug had been in the can and stuck to the top of my mouth. I kept my tongue as to block my throat so the bug wouldn't get down my throat. Trying to pry the bug out with my fingers, blood started to run down my hand and puddle at my feet. The bug seemed to dig in tighter the more I tried to get it loose. Soon, I was running out of air. *Lord help me*, I thought. The bug came loose at the very thought. I spit blood out of my mouth, and there was no bug at all. Tom and Debbie had been in a panic during the ordeal. It would appear that God hears our very cry for help, even when it's not verbal. Satan wanted me to shut up, I guess.

A few days later, I was over at the farm. My sister had a picture of Jesus in a very nice frame. She gave it to me as I liked it so much. I had been washing clothes down in the basement. For some reason, the washer got stuck on a cycle. I had been telling Ma why I thought Jesus was coming soon. My cousin stopped over for a visit to talk to Ma. As they were talking out on the porch, I had a very strange feeling as though something was trying to squash my spirit like a pop can. I got so uncomfortable I had to leave and get back to the camper. I left my clothes there. It had been two hours since I put them in the washer. Arriving at the camper, I put the picture of Jesus in the chair. It just so happened it was facing the doorway. I was busy getting my coffee ready for the next day when I heard someone step up on the camper step. The door opened and without looking up, I told my brother to come in. When I looked, no one was there. "In Jesus's name, be gone," I said. The door closed by itself. I have to say I was shook up. All that night, I'd wake up, read the Bible, and pray. The morning came, and I was exhausted. The preacher had been right to expect resistance. I'd forgotten those words.

That day, I left to head back to Montana. I needed to stop by my cousin's house on the way. I got a little sleep there and visited for a while. My uncle Albert had given me fifty dollars. On the road, I met a kid who was digging in the trash. I gave him ten bucks so he could get food. He had too much stuff to get in my little car, so I couldn't give him a ride. When I got to Jamestown, North Dakota, I got a room. After I got cleaned up, I was praying and asked God what he wanted me to see here. Opening my Bible, it opened up to Joel. Joel happens to be the end-time prophet. The timing had been perfect. I arrived one week later and in time to go to the Bible study at the church where I had slept for a few hours.

The time came when Bible study was to begin. I was a little nervous as I walked in. There were only about five people there. I helped myself to coffee and sat down. The pastor asked me to grab a stack of papers, which were about two inches thick and stapled together. I put my name in the proper space. I was then asked, "Who is your best friend?"

"My best friend is Jesus," I replied.

"Oh no, we don't mean that. Who is your best friend, and what do you like about him?" they asked again.

"Jesus is my best friend, and what I like about him is his love and truth," was my reply. After that question, I was slightly angry. It must have been noticed because we then switched to reading the Bible. As my turn came to read a verse, my speech was louder than normal. I thought, *These people need to hear the word.* At the end of Bible study, one person acted as though he wanted to tell me something. I noticed and asked him to come for coffee. At the restaurant, we discussed the paperwork.

"Kinda dry, wasn't it?" my friend said.

"Dry," I said, "that's like trying to feed you a bowl of sand." The only thing we could come up with to explain that paperwork was that they were trying to teach salvation on earth. You don't need God anymore. We'll teach you salvation. *This must be the one religion that Grandma warned me about*, I thought. After we ate, we got together and studied the Bible some more. My friend was a true Christian. I said my goodbyes and headed down the road.

I came up on a rest area, which also had a small welcome center. I was looking for a map of the Indian Reservation in the Dakotas. I didn't have any luck finding one, but something drew my attention to a book on the shelf. For some reason, I was prompted to take it with me. I threw it up on the dash and gave it little thought. I'm not a big book reader. I only study the Bible. On the way back, I stopped at Sitting Bull's gravesite. I missed the whole road and had to get directions back to it. There wasn't much at the sight. A flagpole was about all. I asked for forgiveness for what we had done to the Indians.

Arriving back at Seeley Lake, Montana, the house felt empty even though people had been living there. It was good to be home though. I was still rattled about the demonic attacks that had happened back in Pennsylvania. I tried to explain to Angie what had happened back there even though it seemed she didn't understand. As a matter of fact, she was very agitated with me. So much so I had to take a drive in the mountains to deal with it. I don't deal well with someone who wants to yell.

Later on, I was to understand why I had this problem with Angie. As I was reading my Bible, I ran into a verse that stuck out to me. When that happens, God is usually trying to tell you something. He speaks to us in different ways. The verse read, "Put those strange women from you." *Wow*, I thought. Angie is the only one I've been with for eleven years. What about the house I could not afford on my income? Turning the page, it read, "Thou shalt not covet thine own house." I have never read those verses in the Bible before. As a matter of fact, I have never found them again. I knew what God wanted. We weren't married, just living together. I prayed about it and asked God to let me marry her, as I loved her very much. I was In the woods at the time and had just turned around to see what looked like a smile in the sky. To explain what I mean, it looked like half of a sun dog, which is the ring you sometimes see around the sun, only there was only half of it and no sun, only blue sky. I did get married to Angie a while later.

As I was walking around the trail, which I'd walk every day, I felt as though God was not with me. I was thinking to myself, *Lord, where are you? Why have you left me?* As I rounded the corner in the trail, I came to a spot where I'd usually kneel and pray. It happened to be right by the river bend. All of a sudden, a little twister landed in the water and took water that seemed to be fifteen feet in the air. It was as if the Lord was saying, "I'm right here with you." I felt humbled and also ashamed for thinking God had left me. Two years later, we ended up divorced. Our home went up for sale as is usually the case when two people split up their marriage.

Now I know how much God wants us to marry, not just live together. The Lord knows I've made my mistakes. I could hear God speaking at times to warn me or to advise me. I finally was doing something right for a change. I knew Satan was working to split us up, and he finally did. As far as the book I'd picked up in North Dakota, I read it and matched it against the Bible. It seemed to make a lot of sense. Nowadays, I feel that Saturday truly is the Sabbath, although I would never put anyone down who felt different. So many people don't even believe in God anymore. A day you pick for your Sabbath is between you and God. We are not to judge anyone. God is the judge of all things.

I took another trip back to Pennsylvania to see my family. This time, I started blessing the farmhouse and also my sister Sherry's house. I anointed Sherry and her family. Then I went down to my niece's trailer, which sat on the farm property. There had been trouble there prior to my arrival. I was getting tired by the time I got there. I had anointing oil and started sealing up the windows and doors. I had forgotten to tell the spirits to leave. As I got to her bedroom, I felt something in the closet. Still, I went on sealing the windows in the bedroom. My brother-in-law had just arrived at the trailer and opened the door to come in. From what I gather, a very cold wind cut right through him. It must have scared him bad because he just left. My sister Sherry told me about it and that he wanted to be anointed again. I did just that. I didn't have any trouble that time back, although I felt the evil spirit had not left the farm. I was to encounter it again on another vacation back there.

On my next trip back to Pennsylvania, I stayed up at my brother Chris's house. It was peaceful up there at his place, as he lived on a small farm. When I went to visit Ma and Pa out at their farm, Pa and I were watching some show on TV. I had fallen asleep, and when I woke up, I could hear him breathing behind me, as he'd been on the sofa behind me prior to me falling asleep. I asked him something, and when he didn't answer, I turned around to see why. He wasn't even there. It seemed the spirit was still there. I told Ma later on that I thought the spirit was still around the farm. She got perturbed by me saying that. "Well, if it don't bother ya, then don't worry about it," I said, being a little ticked off myself at her response. A few months after I got back, I was talking to Ma on the phone. I could hear some static as we talked. To Ma, she could hear someone breathing and wondered if the neighbor was on the phone doing it. It seemed to me God wanted her to know something was still wrong.

The day came when someone made an offer on the house. It was lower than what we were asking, so I didn't consider it. Angie was living in a camper behind the house for a few years already. The housing market was way down, and I was surprised that we had an offer at all. Angie and I were on a friendly basis at the time although there was no chance of getting back together. Then came a second offer that was also too low. By this time, I had enough of the game. Our sale price was way low already. The third offer came up to our lowest sale price, and Angie needed her money, so we sold the house. We didn't have any problems with the money part of splitting up. At first, I put some stuff in storage but decided to get rid of a lot of it. Why pay for storage?

A friend of mine had to have an eye operation in Missoula and needed a person to drive after the operation. While my friend was being operated on, I decided to walk up the street to see how much an engine for my wood splitter would cost. Halfway there, I looked to the side, and a person in a wheelchair was sitting along a side street. He also had a Saint Bernard dog with him. I walked over to talk to him. You could feel the spirit just pour from him. He was telling me about Jesus. Come to find out his name was Jim, and his dog's name was Love. I took care of my business and hurried back to the hospital. Dalton was just getting around after his operation.

A few weeks later, Dalton needed to get an operation on his other eye. I went down with him again. This time, I looked up Jim to see if he needed a vehicle. I knew where a handicapped van was and who had it. Jim seemed interested. No sooner had Dalton and I got back to Seeley Lake than I ran into the person who had the van. Right after I left Dalton's place, they pulled right behind me. I had prayed that they would take five hundred dollars for the van. As I asked that person how much he needed for it, he said five hundred dollars. It came right out of his mouth! The van was worth a lot more, as it had an electric ramp for his wheelchair. The passenger seat also was removable, as you could put your chair up front. We got the paperwork out of the way in a few days. The van had one small problem; one taillight had a short. The person who sold the van wanted it fixed before it left. As we were working on it, the driver's door closed as though by itself, and the taillight started working. "I guess the Holy Spirit is driving," I said. The pastor drove the van down to Missoula, and I followed in my truck. When we got the van to Jim, he told us he'd been praying for a vehicle for about a year. Not only that, but he needed the seat removable so Love could sit beside him as he drove. God sure answered his prayer right to a tee. Jim had been riding trains and spreading God's word around when he lost his legs. He had jumped into a box car that had the bottom removed, and his legs were severed and cauterized during his accident. That's the only thing that kept him alive. While he was lying in the hospital, he heard another voice say, "What do you think of who you serve now?" That cinched it for him. He now knew that the devil was trying to turn him from God.

A few months later, I got everything settled and headed back to Pennsylvania. I had no desire to stay there but needed to drop off some things for my brothers. My brother Chris gave me a motor home to take back out west. I really didn't want to take it but had nothing else to drive. It sure did use a lot of gas. I came back out to Montana and camped down by the river, just a few miles from Seeley Lake. The pastor gave me several Bibles to take along on my trip. I passed out a few Bibles and put a few in laundry rooms along the way. It started getting very cold, and the heater in the motor home didn't work. Not much did work in it, I was to find out. I headed down to Salt Lake City. I figured if anyone could get things working in the motor home, Tom could. I had to move it around each night so as not to get in trouble having it parked in one place. Tom didn't get anything working, so I decided to get rid of it. If he couldn't get it fixed, no one could. I felt bad as my brother had paid a lot for it years ago. I drove it down to Quartzsite, Arizona, and gave it to a kid who needed it. As long as he could plug it into a power source, he'd be okay. I gave a bunch of food and other things to some friends I met in Arizona. We had been worshipping on Saturdays at their campsite. I pray they have found a place to live and work. May God bless them and keep them safe.

I'd been towing a VW all the way down there and used that when I left. After leaving there, I headed across Interstate 40 through Arizona and New Mexico. I passed through Amarillo, Texas, where I'd hurt my back years ago when I was driving long haul. I thought I'd see a friend in Grove, Oklahoma, so I stayed at my friend Ilia's house for a few days. It was good to see her. She helped me when I'd been going through my divorce. Ilia always had a way of making you laugh. May God bless her and family. While I was there, we had a slight earthquake. It had been a long time since I felt one. I don't really care for them much. May God be with those people who go through the strong ones. I liked Grove. The people seemed very nice, and it was by a large lake. A friend of mine named Ron Palmer invited me to stay the winter at his place down in Ozark, Alabama. I accepted his invitation and was on the road again, this time to Alabama.

After arriving in Ozark, I unloaded the VW. It felt good to finally have a room to sleep in instead of the tent. There's not much room in the VW. Ron was very nice to me, and he showed me around the surrounding area. We had some good conversations as he also was well traveled. Ron's neighbor worshipped God on Saturday, so I started having Sabbath with them. By this time, I was convinced God wanted me to observe Saturday as the Sabbath. I've been doing so ever since.

I'd been having trouble with my lungs since living in Montana. It would seem I was exposed to asbestos in the military, though no doctor would explain this to me. Trying to get help, Ron and I went over to Montgomery, Alabama, to the VA. We were there for about twelve hours, and I still didn't get any explanation as to why my breathing was impaired. It had come on suddenly, and the VA in Montana had put me on massive doses of ibuprofen. Thinking it might have been the wood stove, I had decided to go south that winter. Even after being in Alabama and the desert, I still couldn't breathe, and I finally decided to head back up to Montana after a few months in Alabama. It seemed it was very hard to get medical help in Alabama, when they don't know you.

I said my goodbyes and headed north. A tornado had just passed through Tennessee, and the rain was just pouring. After that, the sunset was just awesome. I'll never forget how the sky looked while I was passing through Tennessee. May God bless those that are caught in front of one of those tornadoes. The sky probably doesn't appeal to them. I drove on 1-57 in Illinois, heading toward 1-90. It was around 2:00 a.m., and the reflection of razor wire caught my attention. Looking off to my right, I could see someone welding in a makeshift plastic tent. I couldn't see what he was welding, as it was too far away. The place was huge, and the fence seemed to go right along the interstate. I could tell it was some sort of prison with vertical windows, which weren't very wide, just enough to let some light in. What did spook me was a smaller building off to the side of the prison. It had a huge stack, which seemed to be seventy feet tall. That was just a guess on my part, as I was driving by. Was this one of the FEMA camps I'd heard about? What was that small building with the tall stack? It didn't take me long to get to Montana, and I was glad to be back.

I stayed with the pastor in Seeley Lake for two weeks. The place I was to rent wasn't available at the time. It was furnished, and the landlord was a member of our church. Karen was very nice and a good landlord. After about one and a half years, a cabin became available, which I still live in. It's a log cabin and has an addition built on. The addition is almost the length of the cabin. It has four good-sized windows, which face toward the west There's an old log building, which takes up the view on that side. It's about five feet away from the cabin. One night, I looked out the window toward the west. Just outside the window, I could see a dark shape standing between the cabin and the log building. It was dark outside at the time, but the shape was darker. At first, my heart started to race uncontrollably. *I'm covered by the blood*, I thought. My heart calmed right down, and I watched the darkness move past the cabin. I had not seen such evil since the military.

A few weeks later, I bought a can of white paint. I walked around the property, asking God to forgive the sins that had taken place there. I also prayed for the place and asked God to protect it. I painted crosses at the corners of the property. I haven't encountered that evil since. I also ask God to watch over it every day.

I enjoy living in Condon, Montana. It has beautiful scenery, and I enjoy watching the animals, seeing all that God has given us and praising him for it.

God loves you very much. Ask him to forgive you, from the heart, not the mind, believing Jesus died for you. He truly is the bringer of peace, and the truth shall set you free!

This book is written for those who are walking in anger, that they may know there really is a God and that he loves you so much. He sent his only son to die for you, that through him you may be forgiven as I was. It's a free gift available to all people. No matter what you've done, all you need to do is believe, and ask for his forgiveness.

Father, I ask that those who read this may bow before you and be saved. I ask this in your Son's name, Jesus Christ. Amen.

Ray's Letter

My friend Ray was dying of cancer, and I knew he didn't know God. I wrote this letter for him to help him understand that there was a God.

Hey Ray,

How's it going down there in Salt Lake City? I hope you're feeling okay today. Have you tried the licorice root yet? Don't think I spelled that right, but you know what I mean, right, man? Ray, you've known me for a long time, and what I need to tell ya is about things I've encountered in my life. We've been friends forever, and you know I'm not a good liar. Don't even want to be. Some things I'm going to tell ya seem out there, man, and believe me, I tried to analyze 'em…like wow, that defies logic. I'm not talking about organized religion. As a matter of fact, they killed Jesus. I'll start with the farmhouse, where I was raised.

Word was the place was haunted, and believe me, it was. What was there was also evil. Lots of times, I ended up there alone while trying to get the work done Pa had allocated for me to do, which was impossible to complete in any given day. When it got dark, I had no choice but to go in the house. I'd hear chairs moving upstairs, and when I'd go check, they'd move downstairs. Couldn't win for losing.

I remember this one time; I could hear this thing walking up from the basement. With a rifle at the ready aiming at the cellar door, I saw the door open about a foot. Sweat was running down my face. It never opened any further, but the stress was more than I could bear. Outside I went to sit in the lawn. Of course, it was dark, so I couldn't see a thing. I'd wait outside for hours till someone came home. After a while, sitting outside until someone came home got to be second nature. When I'd be trying to sleep, I'd hear one too many breathing or snoring people. Not only that, but a nasty smell started to invade my room, like something rotten. Let me tell ya, man, it sure wasn't my socks.

Ma got me a cross and the words I needed to say to drive this thing away: In the name of Jesus Christ, I command you to leave here. Man, do they run! You've heard me say these words because they were after you when I was down there. I watched them jump off you and fly to a comer of your camper. May God bless you, protect you, and heal you, Ray. Anyway, on with my story.

When I was little, I had this real vivid dream. I was outside on the farm, and this voice from the sky called my name. The ground started shaking something terrible. I started running for all I was worth to get away. The dream ended, but I can never forget it. I know now what it was all about. God wants me to do something. I don't know what it is yet, but I'm sure I'll find out. I think he wants me to witness about him, which I'm doing right now.

You met my brother Tom. He and I decided to go to a cemetery to scare our girlfriends. The place was called White Cross. We found out why. We went there first to make sure we knew where it was. When we got there, a big bright cross was at the entrance. You couldn't miss it. Cool, let's get the women and scare them. When we got back, the cross was gone. I got out of the car, and going over where the cross had stood, I found a stump of concrete. Thinking someone had just taken it, I put my hands on it. It was old and crumbly. All of a sudden, it hit me. Someone didn't just take it. This concrete was old! I jumped in the car and said, "Let's get out of here!" I was the one who got scared.

There was a time my grandma and some other relatives and I went to see a preacher about forty miles away. While we were there, Grandma and a bunch of other people started talking in tongues. When they talked to God, they used a different speech. I was standing in the middle of them when this cloud started to come over us. I was wondering, *What is this?* noticing the man up front who seemed to be in charge. He motioned to another who left the front of the building and seemed to check the rooms behind us. He came up front to the other man and shrugged, like there's no fire. It was the Holy Ghost who came over us in a cloud. It says in the Bible, where two or three are gathered together, there will God also be. I got to see it firsthand. My grandmother Bessie was an awesome Christian. She often talked in tongues when she prayed. Bessie took me aside when I was small and told me to watch for a one-world government and one church. She said that was the beginning of the end of the world. If you look around today, you'll hear of globalization or a global economy. Looks very close.

Ya know, I had a real good friend, Jim Levan. He was very good on a bike. We were to go on a road trip one summer. That spring, he was killed in a wreck. It really broke my heart. I was sixteen at that time. I was a pallbearer, and when I carried him, this strange feeling of peace came over me. I didn't understand back then, but now I know. Not only that, but the night we buried him, I watched a ball of light going straight up in the sky. Jim and I wanted to bike cross country. After the service, I took my bike cross-country. Of course, you know that.

When I was in the navy, I had another shock. I always told it the way it was about things on the farm and how it was haunted and all. A friend from the service confided in me about reading from this book years earlier. It seems his friend knew of it and had it in a cave somewhere. He could read Latin, which the book was written in. His friend told him if anything happened, just throw the book down and it would stop. They had a chair there in the cave, which he was sitting on while he read the book. It started to raise him and the chair in the air. He, of course, threw the book to the ground, and it stopped. He only told me, thinking the rest of the crew would think him nuts. Months later, I was returning from watch. It was around 4:00 a.m. I was so tired all I wanted to do was sleep. Passing by his rack, a laugh came from his bed. It was so hideous and evil no person could have voiced it. The feeling that came with it made my hair stand on the back of my head. Man, was I scared. I left the area shaking something terrible. Later I returned to try to get some sleep. I pulled the blanket over my head real tight and shook myself to sleep. Come morning, I told him about it. He got very depressed. The times I almost got killed didn't even scare me as bad as that.

Even after the service, I was sleeping at the farm one time, and that entity got after me again. Ma was watching my chest as I inhaled and exhaled as I was on the couch sleeping. She freaked out because the breathing didn't match my chest movement. Back in Utah, Tom and I rented this house on 801 Simpson Ave. Nobody was living in it at the time. It didn't take us long to find out why. Everybody knew it was haunted, except us—things banging around and odd noises. Some guy came to the door and asked if we were having trouble there. I asked him, "How did you know?" He stated, "just talk to her and she'll quit banging around." He wouldn't come in the door though. As time went on, that's exactly what I did. She wasn't evil though. I decided to try and help her in some way. Didn't know how though. As it happened, I was down in the dumps real bad. I was thinking about what we'd done to Jesus on the cross. Forgive us and me, Father. All of a sudden, all my worries and doubts were gone. It was as though the whole world was taken from my shoulders. I was on my knees, just bawling. It seemed I couldn't get low enough in front of the Father. Oh, what a feeling, to know everything will be all right. To know God's love is so awesome! All we need to do is just ask. Father, I know I'm a sinner, but please forgive me, in Jesus's name. The way it turned out, not only was I forgiven, but the lady in the house was gone. Hopefully, to heaven with Jesus.

Years ago, my uncle Kenny had a heart attack. He was in the hospital when I went to see him. Before I got there, I asked God to give him my heart. I loved him that much. God heard my plea and healed him. The doctor couldn't believe it. He said Kenny had a heart of a twenty-year-old. Years later, he did die, but of cancer. I was living here at the time. I went back to see him, but he died before I could get to him. When we buried him that night, I saw another ball of light going straight up into the sky, just as when my friend died. Now I know what I'd seen before; his soul was heading to God.

When I was here about four years ago in this house, I had this dream of a group of people waving or motioning for me to come to them. It was real vivid and happened two nights in a row. Then I knew God wanted me to go to church. So I did, and then I got baptized. After that, things really started to happen. I got a thirst to learn more about Jesus. I had another vivid dream. Clouds were flying by me, and I came to a clearing. Jesus and I were standing there. All of a sudden, I was in me, looking at him. Jesus was beautiful, standing there all in white. Around us were these white crosses, sitting on racks. I could only see maybe three crosses deep because of the clouds or fog. Jesus asked me if I would pick up my cross and follow him. "Yes," I said. Jesus picked one up on his shoulder and started walking away. Picking mine up, I turned to look at him. All I could see was the bottom of his sandals as he was walking through the fog. I started to run after him so I wouldn't lose him. That was the end of the dream, but I'll never forget it. That's why the cross is in front of the house. As long as I live here, that cross will stand there. A lady by the name of Fran Lance came to visit our church. She was a prophetess. God would talk through her, and she would interpret. Angie was there with me. As she informed us what God wanted us to know, I was hearing a male voice talking to me. God told me, "You're late," and I was. I wanted to crawl under the chair. He then said, "I know you really don't like people and you'd rather go up into the mountains and go fishing (This was exactly what I had planned.), but there's something I want you to do. These people need miracles to believe." So out the window went my plans. I'm not going without him. I pray he'll still have me. After Angie and I got married, while we were on vacation, someone was around the house stealing wood and doing other things. When I got back, I was mad and went down the neighbors to confront and fight him. Later on, while I was hunting, I forgot my keys in the truck. I was about a half mile away from it when I realized what I'd done. Again that same voice said, "Aren't you afraid someone will steal your truck?" I didn't know how to answer, and it went right over my head. Later on, I realized what God had meant: don't worry about material things.

Three or four years ago, God poured his spirit upon the earth. People were coming to God in droves. Missionaries around the world were speaking of it. People in church were having dreams at home and telling of them. One man had the same dream as his son the same night. It was about missiles flying over his head. He then realized it was the US being bombed. I had two visions. One was as I was walking the dogs around the trail, I was thinking about my uncle

Jim who had died, and I wondered if he had gone to heaven. In the clear blue sky appeared his name as though God typed it with a cloud, using it for ink. As I was thinking, *Will I ever make it to heaven?* the word *come* appeared in the sky. The next vision I had was here at the house. Rusty and I were working on Angie's car out back. I happened to look over toward the bush to the north. I saw a person in a robe, walking in his bare feet. I only saw him from the waist down because I was looking at his feet, thinking, *That's got to be hard on the feet. There's a lot of thistles out back.* He then disappeared. In the Bible, it tells of these things happening. In Joel 2:28, it says, "And it shall come to pass afterward that I will pour out my spirit upon all flesh, and your sons and your daughters shall prophesy, your old men shall dream dreams, your young men shall see visions." (These things are a prelude to the end of days.)

A few years ago, I drove back to Pennsylvania to tell my family about all these things and to let them know that time is getting short. Before I even left, the pastor at our church told me to expect resistance. When I got there, I was telling my brother and niece at my brother's house. I was staying in his camper. I took a swig of pop Ma had given me, and it felt as though a bug had been in the can and was now in my mouth. I didn't want to let it down my throat, so I kept it closed with my tongue. The bug seemed to clamp to the top of my mouth. I tried to pry it off and out with my fingers. Blood started to run down my hand and puddle on the ground. My brother Tom got real concerned, but I couldn't say anything, or the bug might get down my throat. All

I could think was "Lord, help!" It came loose, and I spit it out on the ground. There was nothing but blood and no bug at all. *No* bug could do that, my brother said. I knew the thing didn't want me saying anything and wanted me to stop talking about God and what seemed to be coming soon. About a week later, I was over at the farm telling Ma and my cousin about God and things to come. It felt as though something was trying to squash my spirit like a can. I got very uncomfortable and left. I went to the camper and started making coffee. Someone stepped up on the camper step and opened the door. Turning around, I said, "Hey there (Tom)," but no one was there. My sister had given me a picture of Jesus, and it just so happened to be on the chair, facing the door. "In Jesus's name, be gone from here," I said. The door closed all the way, and the thing was gone. I was kinda shook up, I'll admit. Boy, do they run when Jesus comes.

I guess what I'm trying to say to ya, Ray, is that there really is a God, and his Son did die on the cross for us. Years ago, Moses put a brazen snake on a wooden stick so all the Israelites who had been bitten by a snake and looked upon it would live. God then put his only Son on a wooden cross and said believe ye on him, and I'll give you eternal life. It is true, and God never lies.

God bless you, Ray!

Your friend,
Gary W.

World-End Observations

I FELT A NUMBER OF years ago that so many people die around the world, and no one ever remembers them. As I had a hard time sleeping because of my back pain, I'd turn on the news at various times during the night. I started to record what I saw. Later, I came to realize that it was God, trying to warn us to turn back from what we were doing. Amos 4:7–8 says,

> And furthermore, I withheld the rain from while there were 3 months still until harvest. Then I would send rain on one city and on another I would not send rain. One part would be rained on while the part not rained on would dry up. So two or three city would stagger to another city to drink water but would not be satisfied. Yet you have not returned to me, declares the LORD.

The following are some of these warnings:

A one-world government and one church were foretold to me by my grandmother. Bessie Brassington was a very religious person and held our family together. She told me when I was very young that this was the start of the end of the world. She knew I'd be here to see it no matter how hard I tried not to be. She told me to remember those words. Bessie often spoke in tongues when she prayed to God. I'll never forget those words. God bless you all.

Before September 11, 2001

- Gulf War: President Bush (older) announces the new world order, people on the road are spooked.
- President Reagan begins move to weaken and abolish unions…at the same time Russia is trying to crush solidarity.
- President Clinton claims we need more prisons. A lot of barbed wire is being shipped around the US. Talk among the "over the road" drivers as prisons are being built… Mistrust of US government grows.
- Clinton pushes for NAFTA (North American Free Trade Agreement). Corporations now can take their business out of the country…as long as they are on the continent.
- Clinton now pushes GAFTA…many corporations can now move their businesses to other countries where labor costs are low and where labor laws don't exist. I'm sure you heard of Nike sneakers, and all of the employees are usually children being used in terrible work conditions with long hours.
- The US government talks about school uniforms. Doesn't China have school uniforms? Sure sounds the same to me.
- Mayor of D.C. asked to use National Guard to help enforce the law. Clinton states he needs to check the constitution to see if it's legal. Idea imposed on the American people.
- Drug tests are now everywhere; you can't even hold a job without having one. You can't flip a burger without one.
- Constitution slips some more. Interstate traffic can be routed off main flow to be checked by police at random. There is no need for a cause to be searched anymore, such as swerving or having a taillight out. (probable cause)

September 11, 2001

- World Trade Center and Pentagon hit with aircraft. Great loss of life, terrorists to blame. Strange fact: buildings fell straight down.

- Anyone who is a political prisoner can be held in jail without cause until government decides otherwise. The three-day law is changed to seven for offenders of everyday crimes to be held without being charged. Personal medical information can now be used by the government when needed.
- President Bush wants to give money to the churches for the needy. Did the government not just take funds from the needy? It was called workfare instead of welfare. To do this will eliminate the gap between church and state. Also, once the church gets used to having these funds, the government will then control them by the threat of discontinuing these funds. Government control will then be the outcome.
- Microchip being advertised on the news and first digital family take implant (mark of the beast). Asteroid comes closest, about the size of a soccer field. Global killer 1.5 miles wide will come closest to earth or hit in the year 2019.
- Whales wash up on the beaches in Maine. Cause of death unknown. Tons of squid washed up on the beaches in California, then removed with pay loaders. Cause of death unknown.
- Dark water…large area east of Florida is seen by satellite. When researched, no fish in the area… Lack of oxygen in the water. There seems to be some kind of moss or something like it underwater. They don't know if this is the reason or why it would take out the oxygen from the water.

February 17, 2003

- CNN—No cash to pay your tithe in church; charge your contributions by credit card. Debit cards are rampant. Many, if not all, states use them now. These cards are used instead of cash. Your funds are put directly into the bank, then funds are deducted from your account, as you use them… No need for cash, or a checking account This is a prelude to the mark of the beast (microchip). The machines are already in the grocery stores. They now read the barcode on food items and other products. Soon they will read the chip that is implanted under your skin. They shall not buy or sell without the mark of the beast. Beware of this!

- It has been brought to my attention, that some churches have a program going where they will teach you salvation. Salvation comes as a gift from God when you believe in the Savior Jesus Christ and you are forgiven. It's not something man can teach you.
- An ice chunk the size of Texas has disappeared into the ocean.
- Fifty thousand Christians killed in Sudan. UN stalls on help. About two million surrounded without food by Muslims.

December 26, 2004

- A major earthquake in the Indian Ocean caused a huge tsunami which hit eleven nations and killed 225,000 people. Aceh, Indonesia was hit the most severely. Sri Lanka was the second highest in fatalities. Tsunamis are not common in the Indian Ocean. Therefore, no early warning equipment was in place at the time.
- Five hundred large squid wash up on a California beach, average weight is seventeen pounds.
- Shroud of Turin (material believed to have been used to wrap up Jesus Christ after his death) was retested and found to be 1300–3000 years old.

January 2005

- Forty-nine dolphins were stranded on a beach in the Florida Keys. (Sure seems like God is trying to tell us the time is near. His Son, Jesus Christ, died for our sins on the cross. All you need to do is believe it and ask our Father for forgiveness.)

March 1, 2005

- President Bush again proposes giving funds to the churches while saying social security is in trouble financially.

March 28, 2005

- 8.7 earthquake in Sumatra killed six hundred people. This earthquake was in the same area as the December 26, 2004 earthquake. An earthquake of a high magnitude happening in the same area hasn't happened in over one hundred years. The aftershock was 6.2.
- Bird flu outbreak in North Korea
- Ebola virus outbreak in Angola kills one hundred people, mostly children.

July 14, 2005

- Solar system seen through telescope has three suns. This disproves the big bang theory, CNN information

July 27, 2005

- Mumbai, India received thirty-seven inches of rain in twenty-four hours. One thousand people known dead from flooding and mudslides. Many animals also dead and floating.

August 14, 2005

- Israel starts pullout of Gaza strip. Purpose is to give the land to the Palestinians, hoping this will bring around peace. Israelis are removed from homes. Pullout date same as traditional date of destruction of God's Temple, which was destroyed twice (Jerusalem). Leviticus 25:23 says,

"The land shall not be sold, for the land is mine. For ye are strangers and sojourners with me."

- Hurricane hits New Orleans, Los Angeles. Katrina is stage 4, terrible flooding and loss of life. One thousand and three people died. Deadliest hurricane since 1928 in the USA.

September 13, 2005

- Hurricane Ophelia hangs off coast of North Carolina for a few days, very strange for a hurricane to set in one spot.

October 5, 2005

- President Bush announces possible use of military due to possible bird flu outbreak. Containment of flu is the reason for use of military forces to enforce containment. Why does this sound odd?
- FBI wants records of public libraries (Patriot Act). Libraries want public to know what is going on. Federal judge places gag order on libraries.

October 8, 2005

- Earthquake in Islamabad, Pakistan. 7.6 very shallow quake most powerful in one hundred years
- Bird flu shows up in Turkey, seems to be spreading. This is what Jesus said about the end-time. For nation shall rise against nation, and kingdom against kingdom, and there shall be famines, and pestilences, and earthquakes in diverse places. All these are the beginning of sorrows.
- Eighty people have died from the bird flu since 2003. They had been in direct contact with birds. The US government is concerned that flu could mutate and start jumping from person to person.

March 22, 2006

- H5N1 strain of bird flu found in Gaza, Israel

April 2, 2006

- Severe drought in Somalia, Africa

April 2, 2006

- Twenty-seven people killed in Midwest by tornadoes. Tornado season seems early this year.

May 23, 2006

- Warning: Bird flu seems to have mutated. Six people in one family have died from the flu in Indonesia. No bird found.

May 27, 2006

- 6.2 earthquake kills 5,400 in Indonesia, 6.7 earthquake in Tonga, an island not far from Indonesia.
- Heavy rains in Pennsylvania causes flooding; no hurricane involved. This seems very strange.

July 2006

- Israel, tired of rockets being fired from Gaza and Lebanon, go to war with Hezbollah. Many rockets are fired on Israel. Air strikes are used against Hezbollah. Ground troops are used on both sides. God bless Israel.
- Highest temps ever in the USA. 100+ degrees over most of the country. Scientists think this will continue due to global warming.

September 23, 2006

- Iran's president Ahmadinejad looking forward to Armageddon. He also is in the process of building centrifuges used to make nuclear materials. He also calls for the annihilation of Israel.

October 9, 2006

- North Korea sets off underground nuclear blast. The US is worried and calls for sanctions.

November 2, 2006

- Iran test-fires missile capable of delivering nuke to Israel. Israel withdraws IDF troops from South Lebanon. UNIFIL forces to control Hezbollah from firing rockets into Israel. More Kassams (rockets) being fired on Israel. UNIFIL troops not able to stop flow of arms from Syria to Hezbollah fighters. Cease-fire very unstable. God bless Israel.

December 2006

- New laser weapon designed in the US that would help protect Israel from rockets has been stopped by the US government. Sale is blocked to secure aid from Saudi Arabia. US seeking help in Iraq War.

January 16, 2007

- CNN news—Saudi Arabia will give the US support in Iraq.

January 20, 2007

- Winds up to 100 mph kill forty-five people in the UK. Warmer ocean waters are said to be the problem.
- China sends up satellite and then destroys it with rocket. The US is alarmed because their satellites are same range from earth and are used for military purposes. (Could this be a test against our defenses?)

January 2007

- Bird flu now in Britain, deadly strain.
- Two hundred thousand people homeless in Indonesia. Water has reached thirteen feet in places.

March 2007

- Wheat from China shipped to the US is poisoned and is put in dog and cat food. Many animals have kidney failure and die. Wheat is then fed to hogs to be used for food. Government says it's okay.
- Thirty thousand people die in Europe due to extreme heat.
- New Mexico—Thirteen tornadoes in five hours; sixteen people injured.
- Honeybees leaving nests, reason unknown.

April 2007

- Twenty-five percent of bees have left their nests, have left honey and babies behind. This has happened around the whole US.

February 2006

- Australia—Worst drought in one hundred years. Snakes looking for water come in contact with people, and many fires are caused by the drought.

August 2007

- 7.4 magnitude earthquake hit Jakarta, Indonesia, injuries unknown.

2007

- Child in US school dies from new infection, which is flesh-eating and resistant to any antibiotics.
- Fires in southern California burn.

January 2007

- New deadly strain of cold flu virus in the USA
- Three thousand one hundred fourteen killed in cyclone; 150 mph winds in Bangladesh, Indonesia
- Millions of seeds stored in Antarctica by all countries (Do the top people know something is about to happen?)

January 2008

- Southern China gets worst snowstorm in decades; dozens killed, major damage.

February 2008

- Kentucky, Tennessee—Fifty-six people killed by tornadoes.
- California—Seventy birds wash up on California beach.
- Afghanistan—One thousand people die due to bitter cold and lack of fuel.

March 2008

- Texas, Missouri, Ohio, Arkansas, Illinois—Severe flooding due to heavy rain
- One hundred twenty acres of ice breaks off Antarctica.

April 2008

- Chicago, Illinois, to Alabama—5.2 earthquake shakes skyscrapers.

May 2008

- Burma—Cyclone 120 mph winds, twenty inches of rain, 130,000 people dead.
- China—7.8 earthquake kills ninety thousand people; many schools fall on children.
- USA—Ninety-eight people killed by tornadoes since beginning of year. Worst in ten years.

June 2008

- Indiana flooding widespread; eleven inches of rain worst in one hundred years.

August 2008

- Russia attacks Georgia with bombs and tanks. USA stands idle (oil?).

October 2008

- Worldwide: Stocks fall; USA promotes nine hundred-billion-dollar bailout for banks to recover stock market. Seems like major move to get government control of banks. (New world order?) If bill not approved by Congress, martial law would be declared (sounds scary).

December 2008

- Movement to take God from presidential inauguration. Forgive us, Father.
- Brazil flood, 116 people die, worst in thirty-four years.
- Washington state—Olympia supports anti-God plaque near nativity scene.
- USA job loss 533,000; worst in thirty-four years.

January 2009

- Israel goes to battle with Gaza. Rocket attacks from Gaza is the problem. God bless Israel.
- Temporary ceasefire in Gaza; Israel withdraws.

February 2009

- Australia—mass stranding of dolphins and whales

March 2009

- CNN—One in fifty children are homeless.
- Numerous tremors at southern end of San Andreas fault; major earthquake in California expected.

April 2009

- G20 summit: China wants international currency (New world order).
- Earthquake kills 275 people in Italy.
- Eighty dead in Mexico, thousands sick from swine/avian flu. Eight cases in the USA.

- Seems the falling away has begun with churches. People are leaving churches nationwide.
- Swine/avian flu affects twenty- to fifty-year-olds. One hundred deaths in Mexico, twenty sick in the USA. One confirmed case in Spain.
- H1N1 flu (swine/avian) in eleven states, alert level 5, outbreak in nine countries.

May 2009

- Canadian man gives pigs the flu.
- Swine/avian flu cases up to 1,516
- CNN swine/avian flu up to 642 in the USA, 1,893 cases worldwide
- Pope Benedict visits Arab country for the first time.
- Swine/avian flu up to 2,500 cases worldwide
- Thirty-eight dead in Brazil, eight hundred thousand relocated due to flooding
- One thousand six hundred thirty-nine cases of swine/avian flu in the USA
- Pope to visit Israel, wants a Palestinian state
- CNN—UN wary of second round of swine/avian flu. Flu confirmed in six more US states.
- CNN—Seven schools close due to swine/avian flu in the USA.
- World Health Organization wants to go to highest level of alertness.
- Japan closes two thousand schools, 130 confirmed cases of swine/avian flu.
- Swine/avian flu cases reach ten thousand.
- CNN—The US burns Bibles in Afghanistan; Iran tests surface-to-surface missile.
- North Korea sets off underground nuclear test.
- CNN—USA has 6,500 cases of swine/avian flu.
- North Korea threatens war if its shipping is stopped.
- North Korea no longer bound by 1953 peace treaty.

- BBC News—Honduras has 7.1 earthquake off its coast.
- Sixty-five beached whales die on South African beach.

June 2009

- WHO to declare global outbreak of swine/avian flu (martial law?).
- USA—Southern Miami thunderstorm produces seven inches of rain in a few hours.
- Australia—Swine/avian flu could force WHO declaration of worldwide pandemic.
- Swine/avian flu in seventy-two countries, 27,700 infected. WHO might declare level 6.
- Swine/avian flu reaches thirty thousand worldwide.
- Israel's prime minister, Netanyahu, states he will allow Palestinian state under certain conditions.
- Three US states report first deaths from swine/avian flu.
- CNN—One million citizens in the USA have swine/avian flu.

July 2009

- President Obama to meet with the Pope.
- CNN—One hundred thousand new cases of swine/avian flu in the UK.

August 2009

- CNN—Global deaths exceed 1,000; 1,154 due to swine/avian flu.

September 2009

- Swine/avian flu in all fifty states of the US

October 2009

- One thousand one hundred die in Indonesia by earthquake.

November 2009

- Obama declares national emergency because of swine/avian flu.
- CNN—Seven hundred people injured in Iran from 4.9 earthquake.
- CNN—3,900 die from swine/avian flu in the USA.

December 2009

- Iran tests surface-to-surface missile that could reach Israel and US bases on Persian Gulf; range of missiles 1,200 miles.
- One hundred twenty-five whales die stranded in Australia.
- Iran seeks raw uranium from Kazakhstan, 1,350 tons.

January 2010

- Haiti hit by massive 7.0 earthquake, twenty-eight aftershocks, fifth strongest in two hundred years.
- Haiti hit by 6.1 earthquake thirty-six miles from Port-au-Prince; death toll over 111,000.

February 2010

- 8.8 earthquake in Chile, over four hundred killed.
- Earth's axis shifts.

March 2010

- Norway's doomsday seed vault contains half a million seeds. It's located in the Arctic, 620 miles from the North Pole.

- Nigeria—Two hundred Christians massacred in Dogo Nahawa.

April 2009

- Volcano erupts in Iceland, scientists expecting more due to ice melt.

June 2010

- Seven hundred fifty thousand people evacuate due to floods in China.

July 2010

- Pakistan—Heavy rains break record; 1,500 people dead, one-fifth of country underwater.

September 2010

- 7.0 earthquake hits New Zealand.
- Asteroid comes close to earth, between earth and moon.
- UN announces position for delegate to welcome extraterrestrials.

October 2010

- One thousand one hundred die in Haiti from cholera, has gone up to 3,600.

November 2010

- Portugal has strikes to stop wage cuts for federal employees and other policies.
- Ireland has strikes to stop wage and welfare cuts, bank bailouts.

- South and North Korea fire missiles at each other.
- Missile fired off California coast; China is suspected.

December 2010

- North Korea threatens war with the US over military maneuvers.
- Beebe, Arkansas—Thousands of red-winged blackbirds fall dead. The reason is unknown. Fish also dead in nearby river. Is this God's warning? One hundred thousand fish dead.

January 2011

- More bird deaths in the US. Hundreds in Kentucky, Arkansas, Tennessee, Louisiana. Also in Falköping, Sweden.
- Fish die in the US; two million turtle doves. In Italy between one hundred and one thousand die.
- Three hundred people die in flooding in Brazil.
- Riots in Egypt erupt, largest since 1977; seems food and living prices are the cause.
- Riots spread in the Middle East—Egypt, Lebanon, Yemen.
  - * David Wilkerson warned by God of worldwide riots (previously).

February 2011

- Russian scientist warns of large asteroid to hit earth in 2036.
- Riots in Bahrain are bloody. Four killed, fifty injured when troops open fire.
- Three hundred thirty-two protesters killed in Libya while protesting against the government.
- 6.3 earthquake kills 160 people in New Zealand.
- Baby dolphins washing up on beaches in Mississippi and Alabama in record numbers. God's warning?

March 2011

- Mideast in unrest, many riots. Leaders are saying Mahdi is alive and to take down the West (USA).
- 8.9 earthquake hits Japan, worst in 140 years. Tsunami thirteen feet high; 12,500 people killed. Nuclear plants damaged. Earth moves four inches off axis.
- Earthquake in Myanmar kills seventy-four.
- Earthquake hits Japan again, magnitude 6.3. Nuclear plants still leaking into sea.

April 2011

- 7.1 earthquake called aftershock in Japan causes leaks in more nuclear plants.
- Earthquake hits Japan again, magnitude 6.6. People are trapped.
- Four-inch hail in North Wisconsin pounds buildings.
- Three hundred fifty people killed by tornadoes in Alabama, Georgia, Tennessee; six states altogether. Worst tornadoes on record for number and strength.

May 2011

- Twenty-one whales get stranded in shallow water. Fourteen die; people trying to save the rest.
- One hundred thirty-four people killed in Joplin, Missouri, by a three-quarter-mile wide tornado.

June 2011

- Two or three tornadoes hit Massachusetts. Four people killed, very rare occurrence.
- Global gay festival held worldwide. How much is God gonna take?

October 2011

- Protests around the country. Oakland protest leads to police using tear gas on protesters. Protests are over job loss due to foreign trade (China and other countries).
- Tulsa, Oklahoma—5.6 earthquake rocks area; no injuries. Strongest on record.

2011

- Thailand—Two-thirds of the country flooded; hundreds of lives lost. Worst in fifty years.

November 2011

- Protesters are forced out of parks by police around the country. Seventy arrested in Portland, Oregon.
- Two hundred protesters arrested in Los Angeles, California. Protesters also arrested in Portland, Oregon.
- Syria—3,500 protesters killed in riots there. Body count now five thousand.
- Iran—Sanctions are placed against Iran due to possible buildup of nuclear weapons. Diplomats are pulled by Britain because of riots against embassy there. Leader of Iran has threatened to use force against Israel and the US.
- California—Santa Ana winds reach 140 mph. Worst in a decade.

December 2011

- Fifty protesters are arrested in San Francisco, California, in Occupy San Francisco.
- Standard and Poor warn of credit rating downgrade for countries in Europe. News warns the US would be affected by this downgrade. (Does this mean a worldwide depression?)

- 6.5 earthquake in Mexico; two people killed.
- Philippines—Storm causes bad flooding. One thousand two hundred people dead, many homeless.
- US contracts are out by federal government to enlist contractors for temporary help in operating FEMA camps. (Are they getting ready for something?)
- Syria—Two hundred killed by government in two days.
- New strain of bird flu called H5N1 has been manufactured.
- Hong Kong—Twenty thousand chickens destroyed after bird flu surfaces again
- Utah, USA—1,500 birds crash-land in parking lot and are killed.
- California—Ten thousand anchovies wash up on shore, reason of death unknown.
- Beebe, Arkansas—Two hundred blackbirds die, possible panic due to fireworks.
- Man dies from H5N1 flu in China.
- Sixty-eight protesters arrested in New York City by police while occupying.
- Thailand floods worst in fifty years. Floods have swamped two-thirds of the country. Hundreds of deaths have occurred.
- 7.0 earthquake just off Japan. No tsunami occurred, and no one was reported hurt.

January 2012

- Cape Cod, Massachusetts—Eighty-five dolphins beached, sixty-five of them die.
- IMF warns of impending financial problems for EU, could involve world markets. (Are we getting ready for a global depression?)

February 2012

- Syria—260 people killed by the Syrian government.

- Three hundred occupiers arrested in Los Angeles, California.
- Washington State has now approved same sex marriage, the seventh state to do so in the US. *Father forgive us.*
- Syria—One thousand people have been killed by Syrian government so far this year.

March 2012

- Forty people killed in the US due to tornadoes.
- USA and worldwide—FEMA camps seem to be completed. (Personal note: I've driven by one myself in Illinois on Route 57. It was huge and seemed to have a cremation building with a huge stack.)

April 2012

- Thirteen tornadoes touch down in Texas, close to Houston; 200 houses leveled, 650 damaged, no loss of life to date.
- US bill to be passed called HR 1505. Will close Northern border of Montana from people using the area. Homeland security would be in charge of forest areas.
- Riots seem to be spreading in the Middle East and around the world. Has the first horseman been riding? Has Christ broken the first seal?

May 2012

- First of the month was called Mayday by the Occupy movement. Many demonstrations took place around the world. It seems people are fed up with the corruption in government and big business.
- Protesters against war are beaten and arrested, three hundred in Chicago, Illinois. Police are using protective military gear. Is this country turning into a police state?
- Students again are protesting in Canada about price of tuition and cuts in aid. One hundred have been arrested in

Quebec. The protests are against a 75 percent tuition hike. Five hundred arrested in Montreal.

- Government of Canada has introduced a new law, making it illegal to demonstrate in the streets.
- Catawissa, Pennsylvania received five inches of rain in half an hour.

June 2012

- EU—Germany, which is in the best shape monetary-wise, has just now had several large banks downgraded by Moody. (Moody is a financial rating company) Is this the start of a global depression?
- Flooding in India has forced two thousand to relocate due to heavy rains; twenty-seven dead.
- Colorado Springs, Colorado—Raging fires have devastated areas and homes, worst ever seen.

July 2012

- Russia, southern Krasnodar region—Five months of rain in twenty-four hours; 171 killed in flash flooding.
- Spain—Seventy people injured when protesting austerity cuts by police using batons and rubber bullets.
- Israel—Man sets himself on fire in protest against government's policy. It would seem government favors rich there also (global greed is rampant). Man has passed away in hospital due to severe burns. Second to die in protest.

August 2012

- USA—Severe drought has caused food prices to rise; expected to rise 30 percent.
- Kenya—Fifty-two women and children are killed in tribal warfare.

September 2012

- Disabled in the UK having benefits cut because of austerity programs. (This will be in the US soon. What happens in Britain always filters to the US.)
- Movie filmed in the USA about Mohammad has enraged Muslims in thirty countries. Riots have taken place around US embassies; diplomat and marines killed.
- China in dispute with Japan about islands they want to occupy. Patrol boats have been sent to sea of Japan by China.

October 2012

- Massive protests against austerity cuts erupt in thirty countries.
- Huge protest in the UK against austerity cuts.

November 2012

- Israel launches air strikes against Gaza. Air strikes kill commander of Hamas military. This is due to rockets fired against southern Israel.
- USA—Hurricane Sandy hits the East Coast. Sandy was almost classified as a superstorm. Sandy turns into New Jersey and New York City, closes down Wall Street stock market for two days (seems God is trying to tell us something).

December 2012

- Pope Benedict XVI has called for the establishment of the World Bank and a new world government.
- UN estimates sixty thousand Syrians killed in civil war.
- Philippines—Typhoon Bopha kills one thousand.

- India and China in dispute about mineral rights in the South China Sea. (God has said nation shall rise against nation in the end times).
- Newtown, Connecticut—Gunman kills twenty children and six adults. Automatic rifle and two pistols were used in school shooting. Gunman was twenty-one years of age, shy and withdrawn.

January 2013

- France sends troops to Mali.
- USA—Month of January has fifty-four tornadoes, second-most in history.

February 2013

- Pope Benedict to resign on the twenty-eighth of the month; new pope will be elected.
- Solomon Islands has 8.0 earthquake; five killed, no bad tsunami.
- Meteor explodes over the Urals in Russia. One thousand two hundred people injured from shockwave. The next day, asteroid passes by the earth. Comes very close between satellite orbit and earth. (It would seem God is trying to warn us to turn back to *him*.)

March 2013

- USA—First round of austerity cuts are approved by Obama.
- North Korea aims missiles at USA, South Korea, and Japan.
- Cyprus—People who have over one hundred thousand in bank have 40 percent of their money taken by EU.

April 2013

- China—Sixteen people get bird flu; six have died. Twenty thousand chickens are killed to stay off flu.
- North Korea standoff heats up with the US.
- US Evangelical Christians have been given top priority pertaining to terrorist list. (What has happened to the US when being a Christian lists you as a terrorist?)
- Iran—7.8 earthquake kills thirty-four; quake felt in Pakistan.
- Two bombs are set off during marathon; 3 dead and 183 wounded in Boston, Massachusetts.
- Bombers are found; one is killed, and one badly injured is in hospital.
- China—6.6 earthquake kills 196; thousands affected, twenty-one missing.
- Bangladesh—Building collapsed, killing over one thousand people.
- France and Spain unemployment reaches new high.

May 2013

- Israel conducts air strikes against Syrian missile sights.
- North Korea launches three short-range missiles from east coast.
- Oklahoma City, Oklahoma, series of tornadoes. Twelve killed in Midwest, nine in Oklahoma City, hundreds injured.
- Worldwide tornado outbreak, largest and most damaging. Three hundred fifty-eight tornadoes in seventy-two hours, 551 fatalities in one season.
- Moore, Oklahoma—Widest tornado in history at 2.5 miles wide.

June 2013

- Central Europe flooding, $16 billion in damages.
- Record monsoon flooding, 22.36 inches of rain in two days. Five thousand seven hundred people killed.
- Nine hundred Turkish protesters arrested by police during crackdown. Protest in fourth day.
- Frankfurt, Germany—Twenty thousand people protest austerity cuts.
- China—One hundred nineteen killed in fire, working in chicken slaughterhouse.
- Eastern Europe major flooding, worst in seventy years. Three killed, seven missing.
- Syria—Ninety-three thousand people killed in civil war since it started, UN estimates.
- Turkey demonstrations against government continue into fourth day.
- Switzerland has storm, winds of 130 mph.
- Singapore has first hailstorm in history.

July 2013

- Syria—One hundred thousand people have been killed according to UN estimates.
- Egypt—Eighty people killed in Cairo during sit-in while protesting removal of president Morsi. Possible live ammo was used.
- Greece—Unwanted drug users and illegal immigrants who are homeless are put in camps, taken off the streets. (Are these the same as the FEMA camps here?)

August 2013

- Russia—Flooding in eastern Russia has flooded farmlands, worst in 120 years.
- China and Philippines also flooded

- Syria, possible nerve gas used by government forces against rebels. US is sending naval ships to the area (possible military action considered).
- UK and France waiting on facts from possible use of chemicals in Syria before use of military.
- Kyrgyzstan—One teenager dies from bubonic plague. Country on alert.

October 2013

- US government considers placing homeless in FEMA camps or military barracks. (Is this the beginning of the end?)
- Freak snowstorm hits South Dakota. Many cattle are killed in weather.
- Food stamp malfunction causes disruption in stores.

November 2013

- Typhoon hits Philippines, 168 mph winds, estimates two thousand dead.

December 2013

- Jerusalem gets snow, also Egypt, which hasn't had snow in one hundred years.

January 2014

- Australia—One hundred thousand bats die from excessive heat.
- Bats around the US die from white nose disease, which is thought to be a fungus.

Corrupt Doctors, Politicians, and Judges

Judge righteous judgment, says the Lord, for you must be judged. Isaiah 40:21 says, "Do you not know? Have you not heard? Has it not been declared to you from the beginning? Have you not understood from the foundations of the earth?"

The information gathered here is not a call to arms by any means. It is a call to God. Here's what God has to say in Zephaniah 3:8, King James version: "Therefore wait ye upon me saith the Lord, until the day that I rise up to the prey. For my determination is to gather the nation's that I may assemble the kingdoms, to pour upon them mine indignation, even all my fierce anger. For all the earth shall be devoured with the fire of my jealousy."

Fran Lances Prophecy

WHEN I FIRST STEPPED UP in front of Fran Lance, God said to me, "You're late." And I wanted to crawl under the chair, and it touched God's heart. God also told me, "I know you don't like people and you just want to go up in the mountains alone and go fishing, but I don't want you to." I didn't hear God again until the day I married my girlfriend.

This is the prophecy that Fran Lance gave to me:

> Father, we just bless your sons and your daughters. Father, now in Jesus's name, thank the Lord. Oh (talking in tongues). Keep calling him, he's come a long way. He's come a long way in the Lord. And, and, *um*, he wants you to look back and see how far you've come. There's times where you think, where you look in front of you and you think will we ever, ever reach a destiny in the Lord where we can relax? And the Lord says, "Hey, look how far you've come. And, and how many you've brought along. You, you've been very, very urn, urn. Well, you know when you bring people along, it slows you down. And, and I see, I see that since that you are bringing people along in the spirit with you, and ah, it slows you down in one way, but it's giving you compassion in another way. Thank the Lord. Thank you, Jesus. (speaking in tongues) And, and, ah, the Lord gives his Son. Psalm 139:5. In Him the end

behind and before you have laid your hand upon me. And you know the Lord places his hand on you. You feel hemmed in sometimes. It sounded just like this. You like to go fishing or hunting, just get out of people's faces. And the Lord said, "I've made you fishers of men." You can still fish for the regular kind, they're the fun kind, but ah, the men are a little harder to catch. But the Lord says, "Son, just as there's skill in catching the, the natural fish, there's skill in catching men." And, and the Lord says, "He has given you many different kinds of bait. To, to bring the, the urn fish in, the human fish in. But there's still some yet to come. And what I see is it's miracles. God's giving you miracles. And when you pray for people even some that, that urn may spend most of their time in the tavern. The Lord says, "Don't be afraid to go in and pray for some." And sit and pray. And you're going to see authority given to you to set captives free. That a miracle is what Jesus used to get them to listen to the preaching. And it got their attention when Jesus raised somebody from the dead or healed them; they listened. The Lord says that same anointing is coming upon the body of Christ, and you're a candidate for it, so, ah, reach out and, ah, ah, thank you, Lord. Oh, I just see a football player just throwing a Hail Mary, that's the only, right down the, from end to end and, and the Lord says, ah, ah, don't, don't live your life so safe in the Spirit. You didn't when you were in the world (laughs), so he says don't do it now. Live dangerously, heal the sick, raise the dead. Thank you, Lord (tongues speaking), and you know you do it natural, and he'll do the supernatural. And, and, um, it's not turned around the other way. Notice what your shirt says on it. Naturally (laughing). Lord, we thank you that you're going to show your Son, that he's (God) a supernatural, but he's just a natural. He'll lay hands on the sick, and you (God) will heal them. Not your Son. His Son needs to know that he just lays his hand on the sick and you'll do the supernatural. Thank you, Lord, oh (speaking in tongues). You hem me in behind and before. You have laid your hand upon me. Lord, let your Son know that deep within. Thank you, Lord, hallelujah, oh (speaking in tongues).

For decades *Fran Lance* has shared encouragement, healing, and deliverance through God's love, wisdom, and power to thousands around the world. She visited Faith Chapel in Seeley Lake in the late 1990s and gave prophecy for church members.

About the Author

Gary Welkom was born on December 31, 1954. He was raised on a 120-acre farm in Pennsylvania. Gary was born the second of five siblings. His older brother was stricken with rheumatic fever that weakened his heart at a young age. This led to Gary having a lot of work assigned to him around the farm. The family also sharecropped two additional farms, so Gary was made to work alone for a lot of hours. The time spent alone led to Gary being shy and timid. He had a love for all things and seemed to have premonitions of things to come.

Being abused caused Gary's love for all things to turn into anger and then to hate. This led Gary to leave home at fifteen and go to work at a granary. He lived above a bar at the age of sixteen. When his transportation quit, he could no longer afford his room above the bar, as his job was in another town. After drifting around for about a year and a half, Gary decided to get as far away as he could, so he joined the military.

Gary enlisted in the navy in June of 1973 and was stationed on USS *Ranger*, CVA-61 V2 division catapult crew. He only caught the tail end of the Vietnam conflict, but working the catapults was a dangerous job with long hours. These working conditions led Gary to end up with PTSD.

Many years were spent wondering around the US, trying to find a place to fit in. Eventually, he ended up in Montana where he was led to a belief in Christ.

God bless!